Working Together

Partnership in the E... Geography Teachers

Photo: Mo Wilson/Format

Working Together

Partnership in the Education of Geography Teachers

Edited by **Brian Ellis**

THE GEOGRAPHICAL ASSOCIATION

ISBN 1 899085 40 8
First published 1997
Impression number 10 9 8 7 6 5 4 3 2 1
Year 2000 1999 1998 1997

Front cover photo: Richard Greenhill.
Inset: Jacky Chapman/Format.
Back cover photo: Margaret Roberts.

Published by the Geographical Association, Solly Street, Sheffield S1 4BF. The Geographical Association is a registered charity: no 313129.

The Publications Officer of the GA would be happy to hear from other potential authors who have ideas for geography books. You may contact the Officer via the GA at the address above. The views expressed in this publication are those of the authors and do not necessarily represent those of the Geographical Association.

Edited by White Line Publishing Services
Designed by Ledgard Jepson Limited
Printed and bound in Hong Kong by Colorcraft Ltd

Contents

Preface

This book is intended to help teachers in schools who are working as mentors or advisers to students on school practice or school experience. It contains examples of good practice which have been developed in partnership with schools and Higher Education Institutions (HEIs) in the education of new secondary geography teachers.

The most recent phase of the reorganisation of teacher training at secondary level started in 1992 when the Secretary of State for Education published Circular 9/92, for implementation from September 1994. The argument was that the quality of teacher training would be improved if students spent more time in schools, if schools were given a major role in the training of new teachers and if established teachers were to become responsible for a significant part of the students' progress towards becoming Newly Qualified Teachers (NQTs). At the heart of the new arrangement is the concept of partnership between all the parties involved, so in schools where heads of department and teachers already provided active support, the changes were not particularly dramatic.

However, many more schools have now initiated partnerships and in these it has meant a lot of extra work, resulting from the reallocations of responsibilities and roles. It has also involved some (not necessarily commensurate) shifts in funding.

This is the first publication of the Initial Teacher Education Working Group, which was set up by the Geographical Association to assist the training process and to monitor changes in teacher training at primary, secondary and INSET levels. Its work continues now that the education and professional development of teachers has become the responsibility of the Teacher Training Agency.

The Teacher Training Agency is initiating a pattern for professional development through National Professional Qualifications. These start with standards for Newly Qualified Teachers (NQTs), which build on the requirements of Circular 9/92, and lead on to standards for Expert/Advanced Skills Teachers, Subject Leaders and Head Teachers. Working with students on their way to becoming NQTs is part of the professional development of all teachers. Indeed, many HEIs now recognise training for mentoring as part of their degree programmes, and so it will be accredited as part of the National Professional Qualifications.

Although NQTs may be trained in school-based consortia under the School Centred Initial Teacher Training Scheme (SCITT) or in the Licensed Teacher Scheme (Ince 1994; see Bibliography), this book draws mainly on experiences derived from partnerships on one of the PGCE routes which the bulk of the secondary geography students follow (Hughes 1994). Its contents depend largely on the willingness of students, teachers and HEI tutors to contribute and share these experiences, which are generally recounted in the panel sections of the text.

Acknowledgements

The contributions were collected and linked together by commentary and suggested activities by Brian Ellis, David Leat (Chapters 4, 5 and 6), Jim Moore (Chapters 1, 2 and 3) and Margaret Roberts (Chapter 7). The whole book was edited by Brian Ellis.

We hope we have done justice to the individual contributions of Juliet Andrew-Evans, Graham Butt, Simon Chandler, Graham Corney, Matt Forrest, Nick Foskett, Sian Jones, Jane Kelly, David Lambert, David Leat, Sarah McGibbon, Steve Mann, Jim Moore, Adam Nichols, Nick Rawles, Margaret Roberts, Tim Ryan and Paul Weeden, to whom we are grateful for their time and efforts.

We hope we have also done justice to the partnerships centred in Aberystwyth, Birmingham, Bristol, Cheltenham, Liverpool, London, Newcastle, Oxford, Sheffield and Southampton.

Brian Ellis

Institute of Education, University of Warwick

Photo: Joanne O'Brien/Format

Photo: John Halocha/Adam Nichols

Chapter 1

Partnerships for training

Partnerships in teacher training have developed from the idea that the quality of training will be improved if students spend more time in school; if schools are given a major role in the training, and if the teachers become responsible for a significant part of the students' progress towards qualification. Naturally, this development is involving more and more teachers taking on the role of mentor.

The ground rules for training partnerships

The ground rules for the new forms of teacher training were set out explicitly in the DFE Circular 9/92. From a school's point of view the key statements are:

1 schools should play a much larger part in ITT as *full partners* of higher education institutions;

2 schools will have a leading responsibility for

   i) *training* students to teach their specialist subjects, to assess pupils and to manage classes,

   ii) *supervising* students and *assessing* their competence in these respects;

3 the *minimum* time students are to spend on the premises of partner schools in full-time secondary PGCE courses should be *24 weeks* [out of a 36-week course].

The Circular also stipulates that school practice must take place in at least *two schools*, although not necessarily for equal amounts of time. In addition, it places the emphasis of training on the development of a set of *competences*, which all students should have achieved at the end of the post-graduate year (Ellis 1993; see Bibliography).

In June 1997 the Circular was replaced by 'Standards for the award of Qualified Teacher Status' as defined by the Teacher Training Agency (TTA). Competences are replaced by 'Standards', which are competences by another name. The TTA claims that the standards are 'specific, explicit and assessable, and are designed to provide a clear basis for the reliable and consistent award of Qualified Teacher Status regardless of the training route or type of training leading to QTS'. They are certainly more detailed and change the balance between subject competency and other generic teaching skills. They now cover: Knowledge and understanding (13 standards); Planning Teaching and Class management (32 standards); Monitoring, Assessment, Recording, Reporting and Accountability (13 standards); and Other Professional Requirements (9 standards). See, for example, the table in Panel 1.1. The TTA states that 'while trainees must be assessed against *all* the standards during their ITT course ... it is not intended that each standard should require a separate assessment occasion' (emphasis added). These standards are about to be formalised in a new DFEE Circular on initial teacher training.

The concept of partnership remains crucial. Although the award of the qualification will continue to be recommended to the Secretary of State by the Higher Education Institution (HEI), teachers in the partner schools should have a major say in how the course is organised and run, and in making decisions about students passing or

A. KNOWLEDGE AND UNDERSTANDING

1. Secondary

For all courses those to be awarded Qualified Teacher Status (QTS) must, when assessed, demonstrate that they:

1 have a secure knowledge and understanding of the concepts and skills in their specialist subject(s) at a standard equivalent to degree level to enable them to teach it (them) confidently and accurately in KS3 and KS4 and, where relevant, post-16;

2 have, for their specialist subject(s), a detailed knowledge and understanding of the National Curriculum programmes of study, level descriptions or end of key stage descriptions for KS3 and, where applicable, National Curriculum programmes of study for KS4;

3 are familiar, for their specialist subject(s), with the relevant KS4 and post-16 examination syllabuses and courses, including vocational courses;

4 understand, for their specialist subject(s), the framework of 14-19 qualifications and the routes of progression through it;

5 understand, for their specialist subject(s), progression from the KS2 programmes of study;

6 know and can teach the key skills required for current qualifications, relevant to their specialist subject(s), for pupils aged 14-19, and understand the contribution that their specialist subject(s) makes to the development of the key skills;

7 cope securely with subject-related questions which pupils raise;

8 are aware of, and know how to access, recent inspection evidence and classroom-relevant research evidence on teaching secondary pupils in their specialist subject(s), and use this to inform and improve their teaching;

9 know, for their specialist subject(s), pupils' most common misconceptions and mistakes;

10 have a working knowledge of information technology (IT) to a standard equivalent to Level 8 in the National Curriculum for pupils, and understand the contribution that IT makes to their specialist subject(s);

11 are familiar with subject-specific health and safety requirements, where relevant, and plan lessons to avoid potential hazards.

Panel 1.1: A sample section from 'Standards for the award of Qualified Teacher Status'

failing. Formal partnerships have been forged between schools and HEIs in which contracts are signed and the schools paid for their contributions. The schools now have a responsibility to assist with the training of teachers rather than just supervising and observing them. (McPartland 1995).

All these changes subsequent to Circular 9/92 have resulted in a diversity of provision in partnerships. It was necessary to define and distinguish the various roles within the partnerships and this has introduced a new terminology, which is set out in Panel 1.2. Different ways in which these roles relate to examples of the diversity of course structures are shown in the case-study panels in Chapter 2.

HEI-based lecturers responsible for geography method courses
Responsible for the HEI-based components of the geography course and variously known as *Subject Tutors*, *Institute Tutors* or *University Curriculum Tutors*. They may have some responsibility for teaching supervision in school. In some HEIs school teachers carry out this role on a seconded or part-time basis.

HEI-based education lecturers responsible for broader education courses
Responsible for the general education components of the HEI course (where these still exist), and may still be known as *Education Tutors*. They are often responsible for liaison with schools over general partnership issues rather than geography specifically.

School-based geography teachers
Responsible for the geography timetable and the day-to-day counselling and advising of the student teachers. These school-based geography teachers have taken over a large proportion of the supervision. They are frequently heads of departments and are variously known as *Subject Mentors, Subject Supervisors* or *Curriculum (Geography) Mentors*. However, it is desirable that the observation of the student teachers should be a team effort by the department, as was the case in many schools under the old system.

School-based co-ordinators, responsible for students
Frequently deputy heads or senior teachers, they are responsible for ensuring the delivery of the school's contribution to the training of all student teachers in the school, including supervision, induction and further professional development. They are variously known as *General Mentors, School Tutors* and *Co-ordinating Mentors*.

Panel 1.2: The new roles in the teacher-training process

Snapshots in the development of partnerships

Many of the issues are introduced in Panels 1.3 and 1.4, which are snapshots of the experiences of the participants in two schools. Panel 1.5 summarises the comments of one group of geography students. The issues raised are then treated systematically in the rest of the book.

'In 1993/94 the school had two students at the same time: one was always very lively and outgoing, and one was not. The department had several very experienced teachers, all of whom feel they have a hand in the guidance process.

'The head of department, as Subject Mentor, saw his job as co-ordinator, to supervise, advise, direct and make judgements about the students' performance. Support was given with lesson-preparation resources and discipline, and there were debriefs after lessons, for all of which one hour per week was allotted. A further hour was given over to discussion of general progress and problems. However, the HoD felt it important that students be integrated into the department and supervision was seen as a team effort. Official observation took place once a week during whole-class teaching. In practice, much informal supervision also took place.

'The Co-ordinating Mentor saw the students on a daily basis, helped by her being based in the same building. Her role was that of a co-ordinator with a brief to deliver the education/academic/pastoral side, as well as to familiarise the students with the school system.

'The early introduction of the students into school meant that they were inadequately prepared for basic lesson and classroom management. We had taken for granted that they would know their geography and may have overestimated their ability to reach the pupils' level.

'The school saw the HEI tutor's role as one of observation and confirmation of the school's judgements. The time when students spent Mondays, Wednesdays and Fridays in school and Tuesdays and Thursdays at the HEI caused time-tabling problems and risked over-exposing our pupils to inexperienced students. It also demanded a lot of time. However, the students were made to feel members of the team and the added responsibility imposed on the school was not really a problem, particularly with the better student.

'Overall, students were felt to bring fresh ideas to the department. The early introduction meant that staff expected a little too much from them, and they may have tended to lack confidence. The longer time in school allowed the teachers to have more control and helps the students to plan and run sections of curriculum more easily. The teachers now see themselves more as teacher-trainers, although the training sessions given were inadequate for the task in hand.

'In 1993/94 the profiling and other documents were voluminous and the simplification of the paperwork in subsequent years has been welcomed.

'The school sees a good student as an asset, but a poorly motivated student is a problem. We felt that the institutes should be prepared to 'sort out' weak students, even if this means pulling them out.'

Panel 1.3: From the viewpoint of a Head of Humanities

The deputy head is General Mentor in a school with a very experienced geography department. In 1993/94, the school had two students for separate experiences. One was outstanding and the other needed more assistance but worked hard and, with the support of the staff, improved rapidly.

'I had a double period each Wednesday afternoon which was allocated to the mentoring role, but also saw the students at other times as necessary. The timetable did not allow much time to observe them, but if the Subject Mentor had concerns, we would find time. Consultation with the Subject Mentor was an ongoing procedure, frequently on an informal basis.

'The Subject Mentor saw her role as one of looking after the general welfare of the students, liaising with staff, dealing with educational issues and problems outside geography. The students' level of preparedness was inadequate as a result of coming into school so early and the tutor-input did not quite match her expectations. She felt that the profile was helpful in that the students would focus on their own progress and shortcomings in line with the reflective process. The simplification in the new documentation was also welcomed. This also applied to the other changes introduced as a result of a review of the first year of operation. One of these was the consolidation of the time in school into a single weekly block of three days. This was particularly welcomed.

'More contact with the Institute would be welcome, but hard to achieve: it would be well above any already timetabled or contracted.

'Bringing students into the schools and supporting them through mentoring helps the staff development and is overall an improvement on the old scheme.'

Panel 1.4: From a Deputy Head's viewpoint

At the end of the course the students took part in a course evaluation which referred, in part, to the mentoring process. They were also sent a questionnaire to assess their perception of the mentoring. Twelve replied and the results are outlined below.

Subject mentors

All the students considered the role of subject mentor to be one of day-to-day help with lessons, class-management etc. Only three saw the subject mentor's role as one of assessment. Nearly all thought the mentors did a good job, with only one or two failing in their roles. Most subject mentors had time set aside for the task. In general, experience matched the expectations. In most cases, mentoring was a joint effort by all members of the department. In others it was a shared experience, but with some teachers giving more help than others.

Co-ordinating mentors

The co-ordinating mentor's role was perceived to be clearly different: it included the theoretical side of the teaching experience, together with general advice and outlining the policy and view of the school. Mentors frequently had time provided and were very helpful, but one or two were not very highly regarded. Their work did, however, match expectations.

The interviewing process was thought to be fair and searching, although some students felt that some questions could have followed even more searching lines.

Overall, the students enjoyed the course and felt they benefited from it. Time was always a problem and now that they are teaching in schools they can understand why! Some students felt that the mentors did not know their roles, despite the training provided in the lead-up to the new course. This will no doubt be less of an issue in future. The variation in the quality of experience and assistance is a source of concern. Two students wanted more mentor help and one wanted more tutor visits but this will not be possible.

Panel 1.5: From the student's viewpoint

Photo: Jacky Chapman/Format

Some practical implications of partnerships

As people have worked on developing partnerships, the practical implications of the new system have fallen into four categories:

- **Co-operation.** Partnerships have encouraged and indeed required the development of co-operative working between HEIs, schools and students. However, this has resulted in changes in the expectations of the different contributions of each of the partners and in the renegotiation, redefinition and communication of the nature of those roles.
- **Good practice.** Partnerships have resulted in the agreement and establishment of good practices for working with students in school and in HEIs.
- **Diversity.** Partnerships have also had to reflect local circumstances, and the nature of the outcomes has led to a diversity of working arrangements and course structures.
- **Cost and reward.** Partnerships have involved costs and benefits for all parties.

The results of research

Research funded by the Association of Teachers and Lecturers (Barker et al. 1995), using information from 142 schools working in partnerships, produced the following summary outcomes from the first two years of experience:

1 Most benefits were intangible whereas costs tended to be tangible. Moreover, while the quality of the graduate intake remained high (a definite benefit), the overall balance tended towards benefits outweighing costs.

2 Major benefits were expressed in terms of enhanced professional development, including curriculum innovation and new teaching methods, increased job satisfaction, more intellectual challenge and stimulus to reflection.

3 The main tangible benefits included support with extra-curricular activities and addition of new resources.

4 Staff with managerial roles were more likely to see the benefits of being involved in the teacher-training process.

5 Schools enjoyed the spin-off of being able to recruit good students as Newly Qualified Teachers.

6 Pupils were not seen as bearing the main costs of a school's involvement in ITE. Indeed, they were often thought to be the main recipients of benefit. Pupil discipline and motivation were not thought to be adversely affected.

7 The greatest tangible cost was the time demanded from teachers.

8 Where time allowances were made they were rarely thought adequate.

9 Payments to the schools were not thought to be adequate.

10 There were some tangible costs involved in providing reprographics and consumables.

11 Intangible costs were identified as demands on teachers' energy and increased stress.

12 Partnership arrangements were more likely to enhance the reputation of a school than to damage it.

13 Students were seen as conduits between schools and HEIs, and this facilitated dialogue and curriculum development.

14 Schools favoured the partnership model of ITE and few would welcome school-administered schemes.

Implications for future development

The contributors to this book were drawn from schools, HEIs and the students themselves. They have recurrently recognised that, whatever structures have been devised and whatever nomenclatures are used, some key practicalities have to be addressed if the new system for the preparation of Newly Qualified Teachers (NQTs) is to be completely successful. This book is intended to contribute some workable solutions to these practicalities:

- Teachers in school may well be asked to assist with interviewing and selection alongside HEI colleagues.
- Students now come into school much earlier in their training. This often means that they have not had as long in pre-experience preparation as in the past, so it is not possible to assume that any student has the basic skills to stand in front of a class and deliver a lesson.
- Students will need to gain some of these skills through observing other teachers for a longer period of time than in the past. This will have to be focused and structured while the experience of teaching itself is gradually phased in (Foskett 1994).
- Students will be in school for longer periods and there is a danger of some classes being over-exposed to students. Rotating classes is a possible answer.
- The school may well have a defined training role in areas such as lesson planning, worksheet design and schemes of work. The student needs to be shown how to do all this and to be encouraged to use a variety of teaching styles.
- The school will most likely be involved in student assignments. This may take the form of helping with a mini-

research project and/or assessing assignments.

- The school has an assessment role that includes regular observation of the student while teaching and written feedback on lessons. This will provide evidence for the student's success or failure, and is therefore essential.
- Profiling will probably involve the subject mentor, co-ordinating mentor and HEI tutor. It will be formative in the early stages and summative towards the end. There has always been end-of-practice report. Reports by the school under the new partnership are even more important. At the end of the course Career Entry Profiles have to be completed for NQTs.
- The school-based subject mentor will have to liaise more closely with the school co-ordinating mentor and the college tutor, especially when the mentor has concerns.
- Schools have a role in the broader professional training of students, beyond the immediate work in the geography classroom.
- The HEI tutor will visit the student and school much less than before. Students will turn to class teachers even more than they did in the past, especially during the second/final experience. HEI tutors will take on a different role, probably with less emphasis on supervising individual lessons and more on general co-ordination.

The role of the geography subject mentor in a partnership school

The Geographical Association survey, and the examples described in the case-study panels in Chapter 2, have implications for the role of the geography Subject Mentor, which include:

1. Being involved in the selection and interviewing of prospective students.
2. Assisting in the construction and content of a geography method course either by active participation or by constructive feedback to the HEI.
3. Providing timetables for the school experience - an exercise which is made more difficult during split weeks.
4. Helping the student to plan lessons and giving advice on all aspects of classroom organisation and management.
5. Monitoring the student's progress and providing formative judgements.
6. Facilitating different learning strategies and research activity.
7. Being aware of the geography subject method course and providing assistance to the student based on this. Some mentors may be asked to provide a formal input into geography training.
8. Providing a structured introduction to observation, teaching, assessment and recording on both teaching experiences.
9. Observing the student's lessons and providing systematic feedback, preferably in written form.
10. Sharing in the judgement of whether students are going to make competent teachers and whether they should be recommended for the award of QTS.
11. Liaising with the visiting HEI tutor.

Photo: Maggie Murray/Format

While the TTA Standards document (1997) does not significantly change the role of the mentor it does strengthen the requirements on partnerships for quality assurance which will have implications at departmental level. Selection criteria now include, amongst other indicators, OFSTED reports, test and examination results, commitment to and previous successful experience of involvement in ITT. Furthermore 'where partnership schools fall short of the selection criteria ... providers must demonstrate that extra support will be provided to ensure that the training provided is of a high standard.' It is now an explicit requirement that 'trainees are given opportunities to observe good teachers at work, to work alongside them (and) ... to participate in teaching with expert practitioners in their subject specialism.'

Photo: John Halocha/Adam Nichols

Chapter 2
Different interpretations of partnership

Common features

To be an effective mentor, you will have to develop a degree of flexibility in adapting to the requirements of your partnership. The case studies described in this chapter demonstrate a number of singularities in the formation and conduct of the partnerships. However, a survey of all HEIs conducted by the Geographical Association showed that there are many common features in partnerships:

- The term 'school experience' has tended to replace 'teaching practice', as it is rather more than just practising the art of teaching geography. Students are expected to become an integral part of the school and take part in all aspects of school life. In the past, many schools and teachers have involved students in assemblies, form registration, sports, clubs, in-service days etc. The extended time in school makes this wider involvement easier. It makes the students feel as though they are part of the 'team'.
- Most HEIs commence their courses with up to three weeks in a primary school. This may be a school in the student's home area. In some cases the experience is arranged in a feeder primary school linked to the secondary school in which the student will have one of his or her teaching experiences.
- Most students then go into their first secondary school experience. This frequently takes the form of two days in the HEI and three days in school. During the HEI-based time, basic teaching skills are covered by HEI staff. Where the school is located at some distance from the HEI, as in rural areas, this split week is difficult to arrange.
- School half-terms are frequently spent in the HEI, and this gives the students the time and access to libraries, resources and reprographic facilities needed for research and preparation.
- During the second half of the year, most students move to a different school for their second experience. They spend nearly all of their time in the school and only return to college for brief periods. The resulting lack of contact with staff back at the HEI transfers the onus of support to the mentoring teacher.
- Students from two of the HEIs visit an inner-city location for a week to experience a contrasting educational situation, and one university has a 'field week'.
- There is frequently some form of plenary activity in the HEI at the end of the course to review the experience. In most cases it is only one or two days.
- In school, the students are given assignments. In some cases the schools are directly involved (Hughes 1994), and the topics for the assignments frequently relate to the school experience.
- Many HEIs have adopted a profiling system which reviews the progress of the students at regular intervals. The profile should monitor the student's progress in relation to the competences/standards. Mentors have a major input here.

- The most common pattern of student placement is for participating schools to have different geography students for each of the first and second experiences. Some HEIs, such as Nene, Oxford and Sheffield, place two students in one school. Others, such as Manchester Metropolitan, draw on a large number of schools and do not have a student in each school for every teaching experience.
- Subsidiary subjects have come under pressure. In some cases they have been dispensed with, while in others they have been retained in a different form. At Liverpool Hope, for example, they are termed 'complementary subjects' and teaching experience cannot be guaranteed under the new partnership arrangement.

Diversity in partnership arrangements

Some teacher-training institutions, such as the universities of Oxford and Sussex, already had school-based mentoring schemes in place before the introduction of the Circular. Subsequent developments in all HEIs have led to a great diversity of pattern in designing partnership arrangements, as the following contrasting case studies show. But although there are differences, often due to geographical circumstances, there are also common features which contribute to success.

The London case study

The size of London means that a traditional HEI-school link-up can be difficult to organise. The school may be a long way from University of London Institute of Education (ULIE) and a Subject Supervisor (Subject Mentor) may seem remote. The already-existing 'area and cluster' system is seen as an answer. This means that there is a local tutor who maintains the link with ULIE (see Panel 2.1). The concept of the student as researcher is taken further in London than in many other HEIs, and the Subject Mentor is a key person in facilitating this research. This link role may help the student to feel more at home and secure. As elsewhere, the school staff make a significant input to the professional studies programme.

London's contribution to the training of teachers is significant because of its size: ULIE, together with Goldsmith's and St Mary's colleges and the West London Institute, trains more than 15% of the geography teachers in England and Wales. Despite this, London is an area where there has traditionally been a shortage of teachers.

The Southampton case study

The course structure at Southampton University (see Panel 2.2) has several distinctive features. One is the pattern in which there are two periods of school experience, both of which include split weeks, spent partly in school and partly in the HEI, as well as blocks of time spent wholly in school. This has the advantage that students do not feel isolated from the university. This new pattern has given the geography teachers (as Subject Mentors) a greater input into the organisation and planning of the content of the geography curriculum course. The mentors may not deliver this course, but are aware of what has been taught and can dovetail their mentoring to what has been taught in the HEI.

Although not unique, the block of four weeks spent back in the HEI at the end of the course is a second distinctive feature. There is a good argument for this because it encourages reflection on the school experience. When such dedicated time is not available, consideration has to be given to how a summative review can be undertaken to prevent the course just 'drifting' to a close. The project work included in this terminal block should also benefit from the experience gained in teaching.

Course structure

'The secondary PGCE course at ULIE involves around 750 'Beginning Teachers' (BTs) across different subject specialisms, working in about 200 partner schools. The course identifies three components: Practical Teaching; Professional Studies; Subject Studies. Each of these is subject to formal assessment and BTs must pass all three. Running through these components, throughout the whole academic year, are three course foci: *The Teacher as Competent Practitioner*; *The Teacher as Reflective Professional*; *The Teacher as Researcher*. These provide the BTs with distinctive ways of working on the course and we expect them to develop skills and competence in all three areas as a basis for measuring up against the statutory competences listed in Circular 9/92. This 'measuring up' process is accomplished through the assemblage of a portfolio containing a number of elements, including evidence of practical competence, research, some pieces of reflective writing and a listing of work done. The research is reported back (in person) to the School Tutor in the placement school.'

Teacher/mentor contribution

'ULIE has studiously avoided using the term 'mentor'. The subject specialist in school is termed the Subject Supervisor. The role must involve an amount of 'showing how' and practical advice-giving, but ULIE believes it should extend further than this. The BT should be allowed space to develop as an individual and feel able to bring a fresh, even critical, perspective to the department's work. Heads of geography (or designated persons) retain a supervisory role, but are also asked to account for themselves to the BTs, whom they should allow to adopt a research attitude to their departments. This can be uncomfortable but, when it works properly, is immensely creative.'

'Supervising the work of the Subject Supervisors in school is the School Tutor, normally a senior member of staff. As well as being responsible for a substantial part of the professional studies component for the school cohort of BTs, the School Tutor shares tutorial responsibilities (including supporting the research activity of BTs) with the third member of the students' training team: the area-based Institute Tutor, of which there were five in the year 1994-95.'

Student (BT) contribution

'Partner schools are spread across Greater London and just beyond. The potential for fragmentation or even the isolation of BTs is great. We have found that an area structure has been useful, whereby BTs are allocated to one of five area bases (each containing around 150 BTs). Within an area, schools are grouped into ten 'clusters', which are expected to collaborate in the delivery of the Professional Studies programme. Each cluster provides opportunities for learning and development, which BTs, with the support of School Tutors, must ensure that they use. It is the arena in which practice is observed and undertaken, and in which theory is created, challenged and developed. In future the areas may change, but the cluster system will remain a key structural component. Each cluster has an assigned Institute Tutor who acts as a link and facilitator to that cluster.'

Panel 2.1: University of London Institute of Education

The Southampton PGCE course is operated in partnership with some 40 schools in Hampshire, Dorset and the Isle of Wight.

Course structure

The 36-week course is divided into sequential phases:

Phase 1 (3 weeks) is a broad introduction to the course and includes two weeks for students in a primary/middle school.

Phase 2 (6 weeks) has three days per week in the university and two days in school.

Phase 3 (5 weeks) involves students being based full-time in school.

Phase 4 (5 weeks after Christmas) is the same as phase 2, except that students are based in a different school from Phases 2 and 3.

Phase 5 (13 weeks) is wholly school-based, with students in the same schools as Phase 4.

Phase 6 (4 weeks) is a concluding integrating phase, based in the university, but with students undertaking project work in school.

Teacher/mentor contribution

The course is designed and operated as a genuine collaboration and partnership between schools and the university. The content is decided at regular training sessions (at least one per term) and roles are allocated between the partners. The geography main-subject curriculum course is delivered in the university by the university Curriculum Tutor, but is planned and designed jointly with the school geography mentors (Curriculum Mentors), who provide school-based tasks and teaching that integrate with the university work when students are in school.

The role of mentors in schools is to provide a range of experience and to assess the students both during and at the end of the course. The role of the tutor from the university is to act as moderator of the assessment process and to provide quality control. This is undertaken through school visits and joint discussions with Subject Mentor and tutors.

Student selection

Applicants are selected for interview by the Curriculum Tutor on the basis of GTTR forms and references. During each interview, conducted jointly by the Curriculum Tutor and one of the Curriculum Mentors from the partnership schools, the applicant must make a short presentation. The decision to accept or reject is made jointly by the two interviewers on the basis of a subjective judgement of the applicant's suitability as a teacher, bearing in mind the competences given in Circular 9/92. Interviews have been held in the university to date, but some experimentation with school-based interviewing is planned.

Panel 2.2: The University of Southampton course

Southampton mentors have a joint role in deciding who is suitable for the post-graduate course. Indeed, the involvement of the mentors in interviewing is now standard, although Southampton uses Co-ordinating Mentors rather than Subject Mentors. School-based interviewing will almost certainly involve Subject Mentors. This joint role gives the mentor a sense of ownership, which was not the case in the past when tutors carried out all the interviewing and made the selection for the post-graduate course.

The University of Aberystwyth offered 26 students a place on the PGCE geography course, and 20 accepted. Of these, five were Welsh-speaking candidates. There are twelve partnership schools, eight of which take two students, the remainder accepting one each. There is only one tutor.

Aberystwyth has two special problems which make it unique. These are:

Language

There is a shortage of candidates who can teach through the medium of Welsh. Because of this all Welsh-language students are interviewed. The university tries to provide a parallel Welsh language course running alongside the English language course. There are clearly specific problems pertaining to the teaching of geography in Welsh to bilingual classes.

Distance

West and central Wales is thinly populated, and there are very few secondary schools. Heads of geography from local English- and Welsh-language schools (depending on the first language of the student) assist with the interviews, although neither of the schools which provide staff for interviews are partnership schools because the nearest of these is 30 miles away.

The distances also cause problems for the course. All but one of the partnership schools are over 50 miles away and the furthest is 88 miles. Therefore the mixed school/university weeks common in other areas are not practical. When Aberystwyth students go for teaching experience, they have to reside in the vicinity of the school. Supervision is also very time-consuming and expensive, as distances for supervisors are such that a whole day may be devoted to visiting one student. Much responsibility has to be devolved to the mentors in the schools, as visits cannot be made more than five times per year.

Panel 2.3: The University of Aberystwyth course

The Aberystwyth case study

Although there are other HEIs in semi-rural areas where distances are a problem, Aberystwyth's isolated location has led to the development of a unique pattern (see Panel 2.3). It has had to retain discrete blocks of school experience and the mentors have always had a strong supervisory role. The University Curriculum Tutor is a practising teacher, employed on a part-time basis. She points out that at Aberystwyth the mentors have an extra responsibility to prevent the students feeling isolated. The tutor still makes up to five visits to each student during the year, and this is helped by the fact that some schools are prepared to take two students. Avoiding 'over-exposure' of classes to the students can then be a problem for mentors.

The Liverpool case study

The account of the pattern at Liverpool Hope University College (see Panel 2.4) illustrates the evolving nature of partnership arrangements. There was uncertainty about mentor roles – a teething problem that reflected the voluminous documentation and limited training possible in advance of the new course. The changes described came about from the discussions within new institute/school working groups, in which both mentors and students were represented. In addition the views of all the mentors were elicited through evaluation forms. This gave the mentors more influence upon the partnership, and the views they expressed led to changes. Of these, the change in the structure of week and term work was widely welcomed and made the mentors' lives easier.

The first year of the new partnership (1993/94) was successful. Most of the students successfully completed the course, and the quality of qualified students was deemed to have matched that of previous cohorts. Nevertheless, reservations existed, and the mentors were consulted through a process of course evaluation. Although the mentors had been trained, they found themselves unclear as to their actual role and tended to rely on the HEI for guidance. They did not always relish the task of taking responsibility for the supervision of the students. The following changes were therefore made in response to the views expressed by mentors:

In the second year (1994/95) the role of the HEI tutor was clearly spelled out as that of a moderator, and visits were to be made to liaise with mentors rather than to see the students teaching.

New schools having joined the scheme, provision would have to be made to train the new mentors, even though transitional funding for mentor-training in the second year had been considerably reduced.

The mentors did not like the timetabling whereby three separate days were spent in school; blocks of three days provided more continuity.

The mentors felt that there should be as much similarity as possible between the Institute terms and the school terms. The course was therefore started earlier by cutting the primary-school experience from two weeks to one week.

In the first year the students had been based in school for the whole of their second teaching experience, which had made access to HEI facilities and tutors very difficult. This was overcome by bringing them back to the college for the first four Mondays of the second experience.

Six geography tutors had taken part in the first year. To maintain continuity, they all visited the same schools in the second year.

Where there was concern about the performance of a particular student, external examiners were brought in much earlier than in previous years - if necessary, during the first experience.

Panel 2.4: The evolution of the Post-graduate Secondary Initial Teacher Training Course at Liverpool Hope University College

The timetable and course content has been harmonised with the post-graduate courses run by Liverpool University and Liverpool John Moores University. The split week will continue to cause some difficulty and the mentors have now accepted that students will not arrive ready to teach. Clear guidelines have been given on induction and student observation. The maintenance of links between tutors and schools has been of great benefit. Mentors know the tutors well and liaise closely. An early visit from an external examiner has proved very successful. Students who appear to be failing are presented with targets and are given time to improve their performances.

The role of the external examiner is much more formative in the new partnership.

Cheltenham and Gloucester – a very different case study

Compared with the previous four examples, the Cheltenham and Gloucester scheme (Panel 2.5) reveals a completely different approach to the development of partnership arrangements. Here much more responsibility is devolved to school teachers and in particular to one tutor, who works both in school and in the HEI.

The Gloucestershire Initial Teacher Training Scheme is a partnership organised by Cheltenham and Gloucester Institute of Higher Education in association with the Gloucestershire Secondary Heads Association. Its first year of operation was 1993/94.

A school teacher was seconded to be both a subject mentor and the HEI co-ordinator for the initial teacher-training scheme for secondary geographers (Hughes 1994). A different teacher took over in 1994/95. He is the senior curriculum co-ordinator in an 11-18 school and is a training manager in the school where he supervises seven students. He has one hour per week with each student and is responsible for much of their assessment. He is also responsible for providing references for the students in his school.

Each school has a subject mentor to supervise the geography student in that school, and one hour per week is dedicated to this. Exactly 25 weeks out of the 36-week course are spent in school (10 weeks in the first school, followed by 6 in the second, and then a third experience of 8 weeks back in the first school). The geography subject is delivered in 30 afternoon sessions by the HEI co-ordinator.

Compared with other university/institute-based schemes, the students spend much more time in school and feel that the new course is a good one.

The subject mentors perform a role similar to that in other university/institute-based schemes. They feel that students bring fresh ideas and enthusiasm and became part of the team. In all schools, much informal mentoring has taken place. As in other parts of the country, providing students with sixth-form experience can be a problem.

Panel 2.5: The Gloucestershire Initial Teacher Education Scheme

Photo: John Halocha/Adam Nichols

Chapter 3

Partnership and the selection of students

Understanding the student-selection process is essential background information for successful mentoring, and, ideally, you may now be part of the process. The problem of selecting students for the PGCE course has always been a source of concern for tutors. Teachers in schools have sometimes been critical of the selection methods when faced with a poor student or, even worse, a poor qualified teacher. Since the directive was made to give schools a major role in teacher training, many mentors have been brought into the interview process and take on some of the responsibility for those who enter the profession.

In this, there is an important cost implication: teachers released for the afternoon need cover, which is expensive. Also, if the interview takes place in the HEI, travel expenses are incurred. HEIs feel the expense is justified if it achieves the objective of bringing the most suitable applicants into teaching.

Partnerships do not have an entirely free hand in the selection process. An initial screening is consequent upon the DfE having stated that the applicant's degree should be mainly in geography. This has to be verified at interview and some 'exotic' degrees may be unsuitable. The candidates are also required to demonstrate a commitment to teaching and not just be doing it because they cannot think of anything else to do with a geography degree. Many students now seek experience with young people before their interviews and may have visited a secondary school on work-experience to find out what teaching geography is like. This *may* demonstrate commitment and test vocation, but should candidates who do not have this experience be penalised?

Lack of commitment is difficult to identify, but failure on the part of some candidates to take up places they have been offered suggests that some at least were hedging their bets. Selection also has to take into account suitable personality traits. While an outgoing personality may be desirable, this is not always easy to assess and some very good students who at first appear a little on the quiet side may be precluded if a personality test is applied too rigidly.

The Circular 9/92 stipulated that selection must involve an interview of all prospective teachers. But interviewing and selection remain problematical. Some partnerships such as Liverpool Hope University College and the University of London Institute of Education (ULIE) attempt to standardise the procedure by having agreed lists of criteria and interview formats (see Panels 3.1 and 3.2). Both these establishments rely on the formal interview, whereas Sheffield University has a more elaborate process in which the selection process takes place in one of the partnership schools (see Panel 3.3).

Joint interviewing was tried at Liverpool Hope University College for the first time in the year 1993/94 and was found to be very successful. When staff availability allows, three people - a subject mentor and two tutors - do the interviewing. One tutor makes notes while the other tutor and the subject mentor ask the questions. Decisions as to who is to be accepted are made jointly, and some students have

The following interview criteria are employed in the selection process:

1 A good degree in geography or a degree in which geography makes up at least 50% of the degree content.

2 Recent experience in a school which demonstrates the student's commitment to teaching and has convinced them that teaching is the career that will suit them. Other forms of experience with young people are valued, such as youth work and sports coaching.

3 A lively, outgoing personality.

4 Enthusiasm for geography.

5 An open mind about how geography might be taught and a critical view of existing teaching, drawn from experience.

A standard set of questions has been drawn up which should reveal how far the candidate matches the selection criteria. Where possible, these are open-ended enough to give the student the opportunity to show personality, initiative and intuitive thought, together with critical awareness of the issues in education today:

1 Why do you want to teach?

2 What aspects of geography interest you most?

3 Have you had the opportunity to see classes being taught geography?

4 Describe the methods of teaching you observed being taught.

5 What other experience have you had with young people?

6 In what way do you think this experience will be helpful to you as a teacher?

7 Describe a teacher at the school you attended who made a distinctive impression on you.

8 What made this teacher such a good/bad teacher?

9 Describe the way in which you were taught geography.

10 If you go into teaching, how might your style of teaching differ from the one you have just described?

11 What makes a good teacher?

12 What do you regard as the most rewarding aspects of teaching?

13 What do you regard as the most difficult aspects of teaching?

Panel 3.1: Interview criteria and questions at Liverpool Hope University College

ULIE has an extensive set of selection criteria. Students are selected by tutors and experienced teachers as appropriate, the choice being based on the following criteria:

1 A good degree in geography and/or related subjects.

2 Other work experience such as adult/community groups, with children etc.

3 An open attitude towards change.

4 A positive attitude towards multi-cultural education, urban education etc.

5 A determination to develop professional skills and abilities.

6 An ability to think clearly and concisely.

7 Good general personality traits.

8 A positive attitude towards equal opportunities.

9 An ability to talk freely and enthusiastically about geography and/or an aspect of geography.

Panel 3.2: Selection criteria at the University of London Institute of Education

Sheffield University has developed a school-based interview scheme. The university selects the candidates for interview on receipt of the application forms. They are then asked to attend one of the 14 partnership schools for interview. Four students may be asked for interview on one day, during which the programme may include:

Morning

- observation of a geography lesson being taught in the school;
- an opportunity to take part in lessons with small groups of pupils;
- meetings with school mentors or university tutors;
- a tour of the school;
- an opportunity to discuss the PGCE course and other issues with members of the geography department, the university tutor and the PGCE students in school.

Afternoon

- individual interviews with the university tutor and, if possible, the school geography mentor;
- a joint discussion with the school geography mentor about the candidate's suitability for teaching.
- Joint decisions are then made and offers sent to successful applicants.

Panel 3.3: The Sheffield University interview procedure

been turned down because the mentors felt strongly that they were unsuitable. This involvement has been extended since 1994/95 and the mentors now feel more confident about the interview process.

With the Sheffield scheme the school takes on a major role in the interview process, but a great deal of organisation is required. The students tend to be surprised by this procedure but appreciate seeing the reality of the school situation, and the geography mentors recognise the value of this involvement. Often the students can become involved in lessons to see if they feel comfortable in the classroom environment. The school-based interview procedure makes it easier for them to ask general questions about teaching and schools. The mentor and tutor can follow up on the morning's experience during the afternoon interview.

Whatever the means used in selection, partnerships will have to take into account both the subject-specific and non subject-specific TTA Standards which NQTs are expected to reach at the end of one year's training from May 1998 (see extract in Panel 1.1). If the interview criteria suggested above are not thought to be adequate to achieve this, even when viewed through the prism of the 'student's self-concept', discussed in Chapter 4, then additional methods may be needed such as asking students to make short presentations to allow them to demonstrate their communication skills, or to bring evidence of work done with children or other groups. These may go some way to counterbalance problematic judgements about personality or enthusiasm. To aid with the consistency of selection procedures between partnerships the TTA is developing guidance on effective and efficient approaches to selection and this should be available in 1998.

Photo: Margaret Roberts

Chapter 4

Analysing the process of learning to teach

There is a view that learning to teach is a simple affair. All you need is a thorough knowledge and love of the subject and someone to copy and away you go; understanding of pupils and how they learn is an unnecessary extra. This is like arguing that trainee doctors only need to know about medicines and medical procedures, the rest can be picked up from watching doctors at work and therefore knowledge of anatomy and patients is superfluous. Whilst knowledge about how people learn to teach is somewhat limited it does repay attention.

Here we look at two powerful models which provide good ways of approaching understanding:

- the stage model of teacher development;
- experiential learning cycles.

Appreciating the *pace* of your students' development is crucial to successful mentoring.

The stage model

The stage model represents the path to competence as a transition from novice to expert (Fuller and Bown 1975, Berliner 1987):

1. In the pre-teaching stage, student teachers are *idealistic,* but essentially *naïve* about pupils and classrooms.
2. The second stage is characterised by a *concern for survival* as class control, subject mastery and lesson planning bring reality and anxiety into their lives.
3. In the third stage, as confidence and competence grows, concern turns to *teaching performance* - lesson starts, instructions, explanations, questioning, transitions and the management of resources.
4. In stage four attention shifts to *the pupils* - their social, academic and emotional needs and the teacher's ability to deal with these needs.

Experiential learning cycles

The model of experiential learning cycles is most recently associated with Kolb (1984). He proposes a four-stage process, which starts with *experience,* proceeds to *reflection,* then to the *formulation of new ideas* and finally to *action,* before the cycle repeats. Thus experiential learning theory assumes that the most valuable source of learning in becoming a teacher is practical classroom experience.

In this process the mentor may be seen as a motive force - someone who continually assists in the student's learning by facilitating or even driving the cyclical learning process by the following means:

- observing and providing feedback;
- assisting the post-lesson debriefing process (reflection);
- helping the student to reach new understanding and generalisations about their teaching;
- planning - helping to solve the problem of implementing the new ideas.

This is subtly and importantly different from the student copying the mentor slavishly, because it draws principally on the student's classroom experience.

The rate at which the learning cycle may operate is affected by the context. Two elements of this, the school and the pupils, will be obvious to mentors, but a third may not.

The school is an important factor: students may be conservative and demoralised just as they may be innovative and inspirational. But, ironically, they do not always find it easy to teach in a school with a strong style because so much adaptation is required.

The pupils also play a large part in determining the students' experience. They can differ in ability and motivation; they can respond positively or negatively to new teaching styles; they can deliberately set out to 'test' inexperienced teachers.

The third element is the student's self-concept. In recent years much has been written about the importance of the images of teaching that students bring with them from their 'apprenticeship as pupils' (see, for example, Calderhead and Robson 1991). There are commonly one or two teachers who make a particular impression on the student, and who are used to form a role image. Students commonly, and partly unconsciously, try to put into practice the teaching strategies and behaviours of the mental models, accepting advice and course information which accords with the image, and rejecting much of the rest.

We all carry a powerful mental model of 'teaching' from our schooldays and it is a basis for action or teaching behaviour for most students. The importance of this knowledge is that it helps to explain to some extent why students do not learn as

'Many beginning teachers arrive with 'naíve' views of the teacher's role and their main worries are 'Do I know enough?', 'Will I will be able to impart my subject knowledge?' and 'Can I control them?' I have the feeling that many of them believe you can only be teaching if you are standing at the front of the class delivering information or questioning children. Therefore, the emphasis is to encourage them to explore the role of the teacher and the structure of lessons.

'The geography subject takes up three-quarters of the teaching while at the university and many of the sessions are structured so that they act as models of different types of lesson. This modelling is reinforced by reflection at the end of the session on the appropriateness of the lesson model for the classroom.

'I am uncertain about the success of this technique. Many beginning teachers appear to find it difficult to absorb this modelling until they have had considerable experience in schools. Why does modelling at the university appear to have limited impact upon them? Is it that they have implicit theories of teaching embedded in their unconsciousness from their own school experience, which take over and are followed because they feel comfortable? Do the students feel that teachers have to be seen to be teaching from the front? Or do they feel constrained by the models of teaching they observe in school?'

Panel 4.1: A HEI tutor reflects on the problems of role models

much from experience and advice as we would expect.

Panel 4.1 contains an account from a relatively new PGCE tutor reflecting on his early experiences in that role and recognising that certain well-planned strategies have not proved effective in practice.

There are two lessons to be learned from this:

1 Don't be surprised if students are unable to follow your advice on teaching – it is not intended as an affront.

2 Do get them to write down systematically the advice that they are given by members of your department, so that they can discuss this later, perhaps in relation to the type of teacher they are trying to be.

Continuing the mental model theme, Panel 4.2 gives a résumè of a student's answers to questions at an interview, followed by extracts from an early lesson evaluation. Certain key words are emphasised, and you are invited to look for the threads that seem to run through from the interview answers to the lesson evaluation.

It is evident from the interview that at the start of the course this student had a number of strong conceptions about teaching and about himself as a teacher: he wanted control and good organisation, but also respect and even liking from pupils. For him, teaching is much about being a performer, and although there is

Answers to interview questions

Good teachers? – 'I had a geography teacher who knew **the balance between friendship and respect. Everyone respected him.** There was a Maths teacher who gave a lot of time and patience.'

Strengths? – 'I am a hard worker and **I can communicate** with a wide range of people. **I am good at organising** and time management. **I can relate to people** and help them out. I am punctual.'

Weaknesses? – **'I am a perfectionist.** I like things prim and proper – otherwise you waste time. I am a little impatient. **I don't like people wasting time when I know that they can do it.'**

Picture yourself in a classroom – 'I am not at the front, I am moving around, **I see it as groups. All the kids are looking at me intrigued.** I give them some short sharp points for them to discuss. Then open up for discussion. It is good preparation for HE.'

What do teachers do?

'Teach students as effectively as possible. Not just talking but using lots of methods. Get kids to think about what they are doing.'

The student's evaluation of a lesson

'I should have stopped the class completely and **laid down the law as to what I expect in my classroom.** I felt that the previous teacher was a lot more lenient than me and **pupils were used to talking and not working**. It was hard to establish myself during this first lesson. I wasn't prepared for this type of behaviour although it was invaluable experience.'

Proposed action

'Next time, get them in and working straight away, i.e. copying something off the board while I take the register. **Lay down the rules of the classroom** – what kind of behaviour I expect – and see if they agree.'

Panel 4.2: A student's personal models of the teacher: matching experience with the student's expectations

some interest in group work it has to be very tightly controlled, with him in command. When the lesson does not conform to this model, the evaluation is couched in terms of gaining control and establishing rules. This accords with moving from the idealistic first stage into the concern for survival in the second phase of the stage model (page 31).

The following suggestions may be useful in this context:

1 Tap the students' views of teaching and themselves as teachers. At an early stage of their school experience, you can ask them for written or verbal responses to a number of questions such as:

- 'Looking back to your own time at school, are there teachers who stand out as being particularly good – and if so, what made them good?'
- 'Picture yourself as a geography teacher in a secondary school classroom. Assuming that things are going to plan, let the picture run and tell me what you can about the lesson. Where are you in the room? What is it like? What do you do? What do the pupils do? How does the lesson unfold?'
- 'How would you describe what teachers do? You can answer practically or more metaphorically.'

Photo: Margaret Roberts

2 With this information you may be better able to understand the way students plan and operate their lessons. You may also discuss whether this is an appropriate model at all. At the end of their practice you can ask them whether they have changed the views expressed in their answers to the questions above. This is an excellent focus for preparing them to complete action plans. At this stage you can also look back at the advice the students have been given and assess its value in helping towards implementing their model of themselves.

3 At the end of the first or second school experience, when students are completing reviews or discussing their school reports with you, offer them the stage model and the description of components of change/growth as a basis for helping them understand the process that they are going through. It can be a source of great solace to trainee teachers if they can put this period of stress and turmoil into broader perspective.

How do students change as they learn to teach?

A major review of studies of professional growth in student and first-year teachers (novices) described a number of components of change/growth, which included:

- Novices become *more aware* of what they know and believe about classrooms and pupils.
- Novices become *more realistic* about pupils. This new knowledge causes novices to modify their view of themselves. It also reflects the growing awareness described above.
- There is a *shift of focus*. At the start of their teaching, students are very focused on themselves and their performance, and typically on their ability to control pupils and run lessons smoothly. As their confidence grows, they extend their horizon to that of pupils' learning.
- They develop *standard routines* that integrate instruction and management. These then become increasingly automated so that they no longer require much conscious thought.
- They develop *problem-solving skills*. Their thinking becomes more differentiated, multi-dimensional and context-specific, so that the novice can quickly read situations and decide on appropriate action. This might be better described as 'with-it-ness', as it allows novices to spot the early signs of a problem and nip it in the bud.

These changes and the stage model remind us that learning cycles are cumulative. Each new cycle represents a development and a new phase in understanding and action. Usually this will mean that performance becomes more skilled and knowledgeable. Further, it highlights the role of the mentor, which we shall explore further in Chapter 5.

Chapter 5

The role of the mentor

Having looked at some frameworks for understanding how many student teachers and NQTs learn to teach, we now consider the many ways in which the mentor, can assist this process.

Induction

The school environment is an important factor in professional development. The welcome and general introduction that students receive here may help or hinder their progress.

There are a number of important factors that determine whether students get to feel that they are part of the school. These include:

- being accepted as members of staff, albeit temporary, and therefore being invited to meetings and social occasions, doing duties under supervision and playing in staff sport teams;
- being asked to contribute positively through, for example, curriculum development;
- the mentor being prepared to question her/his own practice;
- the students using the staff-room and therefore coming into contact with the staff.

Panel 5.1 illustrates many of the formal measures that can be carried out to make a student feel at home in a school and department. Remember that every school is different, so you must tailor the induction process accordingly.

At an informal level, students are inducted indirectly into ways of working. A variety of expressions, including school climate, ethos and culture, have been used to describe the context in which students and teachers work. These influences can be subtle or full-frontal.

One of the most obvious characteristics can be the existing teaching style within the department, although often there will be no overall departmental style. The case study extract in Panel 5.2 illustrates the impact that a department may have on a student.

It is clear from this extract that the student had been shifted in a particular direction as a response to the school context. What is less clear is whether this change will be permanent. It is conceivable that should he get a job in a school where didactic styles predominate, he may revert to his original model. Permanent change in teaching style is very hard to achieve. This example makes clear the value of using mentoring sessions to probe beneath the surface of classroom performance.

Here is one way of exploring these issues. You will need to have the confidence of the student if he/she is to reply honestly. Just pick the right moment and ask the following questions:

1. How would you describe the type of geography taught in the department (regional, schematic, enquiry-based, issue-based, work-sheet-based, textbook-based etc.) and how would you describe the style of teaching?
2. What influence do you think this has had on you?
3. What constraints do you think the department places on your teaching?
4. What would you prefer to be different?

'As an **initial stage** I allocate a time slot to talk to the student about our expectations and ask questions in an informal manner. We jointly identify common ground and issues that we need to be aware of, and deal with basic questions such as school location, start times and dress code. While some advice is given, the overriding guidance is for the students to adopt a manner and appearance they are comfortable with and which fits in with that of the school.

'Student induction to the school as a whole is managed by our Professional Tutor. The students are also presented with a 'quiz' sheet on the **school**, which requires them to talk to the school community and introduces them to the plethora of terminology specific to the institution.

'In the **department** area the students are given a folder containing most of the documentation they will need to consult during their time in school. It is indexed and covers information including faculty staff, rooms, location of resources, departmental policies, syllabus extracts, schemes of work for ongoing topics, class lists and a timetable of their attached classes. Students are also informed of meetings they will be required to attend.

'The students are then introduced to the **key members of staff** with whom they will be working. This also includes library, resource, IT and other support staff who can provide a lot of additional help. I feel it is essential for students to appreciate that colleagues' first priority is to the large number of pupils that they teach; consequently, students should seek support in as appropriate and sensitive manner as possible.

'A further stage is to introduce the students to the **resources** and filing systems that the department operates. Once this is done, students need time to familiarise themselves by accessing resources for particular schemes of work.

'The next phase of induction takes students into the **classroom**, where they meet their attached groups. Here they progress through structured observations, supporting individual pupils, working with pairs and groups, team-teaching and on to whole-class teaching. The pace of this programme is tailored to meet the needs of the student. With geography students it is also essential to develop their sense of place in relation to the school's locality. This is achieved by involving them in local fieldwork activities including practical map-work exercises in the school grounds, a neighbourhood study, and A-level fieldwork within the region.

'Throughout the induction period and the initial teacher-training period as a whole, it is vital to establish and maintain clear **communication routes**, as well as formalised times to meet and discuss prearranged agendas.'

Panel 5.1: A school mentor's approach to inducting a student

Developing classroom skills

Having a reasonable degree of classroom control is a necessary condition for inexperienced teachers. Without control, everything is immeasurably more difficult. Control and survival are the second stage in the model of development (see the previous chapter), and growth may to some extent be halted here if control is not established. Student teachers are usually anxious to start teaching, so there is a fine line between making them over-anxious by holding them back and destroying their confidence through early failures. Useful general advice is usually available within the HEI part of the course, but subject mentors can play a vital role in speeding up the acquisition of

The departmental viewpoint

An HEI tutor reflects on the impact of a geography department on a new student:

'The department in which this student gained much of his experience had, in the view of the course tutor, real coherence and identity, incorporating factors such as:

- a physical base, consisting of three rooms and an office where the teachers spent much of their time and talked continually about teaching;
- a detailed scheme of work;
- an agreed approach to teaching and learning in the department.

'This last aspect could be seen in the lessons, discussions and the exam syllabuses chosen by the department. The approach emphasised the active involvement of students in 'enquiry-based learning' – setting tasks which encouraged them to analyse geographical issues and to make their own decisions about resolving them. The **university tutors** both had personal philosophies that included enquiry-based learning as a central component. Furthermore both believed in the importance of student teachers developing their own professional judgment.'

The student's viewpoint

The student, in a recorded extract of a mentoring session, comments on the effect of all this:

'At the start, in the university, we looked at different teaching styles. I think we'd done some sort of questionnaire or something – some ranking. And I think I was one of the most didactic of the whole group, in my head anyway. I was distancing myself from the enquiry approach and open learning ... but I think the university and the department here really makes me learn by way of an enquiry. I ask myself questions ... I feel like I'm in a time of transition. Recently I've started to move away from being so didactic. At first, I thought I ought to do something a bit different, so I was doing an enquiry-based approach because I thought I should. But it's only recently that I've started thinking 'Yes, it really works; I can use that.' I think I'm still quite keen to teach from the front ... but I think I'm gradually moving away from that. I don't know how far I'll go before I stop, or come back.'

When asked about the influences on how far he might go in that school or elsewhere, the student clearly identified the scheme of work, which had a particularly strong character. When asked about why he thought he started with a disposition towards didactic styles, he replied, 'From the schools that I'd been to, and the teaching that I'd had.'

Panel 5.2: The impact of a geography department on a new student

these skills in the specific context of their school.

One mentor's view of the implementation of that role is outlined in Panel 5.3. When considering this approach, bear in mind that much seemingly good advice will be ignored if it does not fit the students' images of themselves, or if it is out of sync with their place in the experiential learning cycle.

'Students need to be informed about class entry, dismissal, teacher-pupil relationships, seating arrangements, acceptable noise levels, techniques for issuing/using resources, marking and homework policies, discipline policy and the myriad day-to-day practices that come naturally to experienced teachers.

'Next, it is important to show that the policies inform the practice. We arrange for the students to witness good practice in action by visiting a variety of lessons and colleagues both within and outside the department. During these observations, students are encouraged to keep in mind the points raised above, but also to concentrate on the language level and the tasks employed for different ages and levels.

'At this point students are usually anxious to start teaching. It is important here to warn them against 'role playing'. Over the years I have witnessed students trying to copy not only the techniques but also the personalities of teachers that they have seen. They need to be convinced that this is unsustainable and that they must project their own character to find out who they are in the classroom.

'Having discussed worries about subject knowledge, it becomes important to provide students with parts of lessons to teach provided they are comfortable with the content. At this point either parts of lessons or small classes are ideal, if this can be arranged. This will enable students to establish a relationship quickly and help them to find out how children learn. Unless unavoidable, it is best for the mentor not to interrupt during these first experiences, but supportive body language and eye contact is very important.

'A review of the experience should take place at the earliest opportunity. Extensive advice exists on how to structure such reviews, but broadly speaking these should be supportive and constructive, and should set targets.

'Experience suggests that students will need guidance in understanding that what comes naturally to them doesn't necessarily come naturally to children. The focus here needs to be on very specific 'command phrases' so that youngsters are clear about the various phases of lessons: very simple instructions like 'pens down and look at the board' are very necessary. Children will not automatically do these things but it may not be automatic for student teachers to tell them to do so. Likewise, voice projection and the use of praise usually need highlighting and then reinforcing over a period of observations.

'Once these basic classroom skills have been mastered and fine-tuned, they need to be applied to a variety of teaching styles and reviewed as necessary. Some students need prompting to experiment, which means that the extent and type of support needed will vary.

'Through all these phases it is important to encourage students to break down their lessons into manageable units for their pupils. This process in itself encourages them to think about the variety of skills necessary in the classroom. Finally, I always try to draw students' attention to their individual mannerisms or over-used phrases in as light-hearted a way as possible!'

Panel 5.3: A mentor's view of classroom skills

Getting to know the children

A recurring factor emerging from studies of novice teachers is their lack of knowledge about pupils. As the stage model shows, their ideas about children are generalised, idealised and often very naíve. Pupils tend not to be thought of as having individual needs and unique views of the world. In the early stages of a first school placement, every effort should be made to close this gap in knowledge.

One simple strategy is *pupil pursuit*. A pupil is followed to every lesson during the day, especially where there is the opportunity to talk to the pupils about the lessons, their reaction to it and what it is they think that they have learned. It can be surprising to hear about lessons from one of the audience.

Your instructions to the student can be detailed or general:

- 'Keep a record of the amount of time a pupil is listening, talking or writing during each lesson.'

The follow-up can be at departmental or whole-school level. If the student has been given specific instructions, there can be formal feedback on the task, but more general questions will also be useful:

- 'What was difficult or negative about the day for the pupil?'
- 'What was stimulating or positive about the day for the pupil?'
- 'What similarities or differences were there between subjects?'
- 'What sense did the pupil make of the lessons?'

Observing the student teaching

Students often expect the observation of their teaching to take the form of judgement about the quality of what has been seen. In the very early stages of teaching, such feedback may be helpful. At this stage, as they inch towards a feeling of being able to do the job, students are very concerned with, and sensitive about, the adequacy of their performances. They want to know how they are doing and even what they are like. They want to have their views of themselves confirmed. So positive affirming feedback can be very useful. Of course, negative feedback can be very damaging, but it may be justified where the mentor feels that there is a serious problem or the student shows no awareness of the issue.

As time progresses, the nature of observation will change. It may

- become more focused on specific areas of interest and concern
- tend towards the student directing the focus and purpose of observation
- become less judgemental, with the data being more objective and open to interpretation (see pages 62-66).

Video helps observation

The observation of students during lessons is fundamental to development. Video is a valuable aid to refining classroom skills. To some extent, pupils behave differently with a camera in the room, but this does not invalidate the exercise: the students can still see how they have functioned. It is their only way of beginning to experience their impact on a class. Video can reveal, for example, the nature of individual personal interactions, use of body language and voice, fluency of explanations and response to pupils' answers to questions. Most schools have a video camera, and if it has a tripod it does not even need an operator.

Effective observation methods

Make a map of the class, indicating where everyone is sitting. Each time the student has an interaction with a pupil, record this on the map. With practice this procedure can be made more elaborate so that the

Photo: Jacky Chapman/Format

interaction can be classified under such categories as 'teacher-initiated' vs 'pupil-initiated', 'positive' vs 'negative', or 'academic' vs 'social'.

Another potentially rewarding strategy is to assess the extent of off-task behaviour. The class is scanned every one or two minutes and a rapid judgement made about who is on task. A total for each observation is jotted down and, if possible, the number of on (or off) tasks for each pupil logged. There are clearly some difficulties, but greater consistency is possible over time. The purpose is not to judge or berate the students about off-task behaviour, but to explore the patterns and causes. Issues which can arise are gender bias, quiet children quietly doing very little, transitions from one task to another, monitoring and scanning the class, and differentiation.

Some mentors are inclined to say that they cover these aspects in their observation of a student teaching. Three points need to be made here:

1 General observation often fails to throw up the interesting patterns that can be revealed by systematic observation.

2 The 'objective' data allows a different relationship to develop between mentor and student, as the student has the chance to interpret the data rather than simply being judged.

3 Students can be asked to attempt to predict what patterns will emerge, thus creating the possibility of an interesting challenge to their expectations.

Structured observation

In Panel 5.4, a PGCE student shows how structured observation is capable of revealing an issue.

This is a representative example of a sustained series of simple structured observations undertaken by the individual student and mentor on a first school experience, and which gradually opened up a significant issue for the student. No

'In an observation carried out by my curriculum tutor, the following comment was written: 'Question and answer in which same boy answers all the questions.'

'In the discussion which followed the lesson, I shrugged off that comment, claiming it was an aberration - a one-off. It wasn't. By the end of the teaching practice it became clear that in the class in question I had failed to learn many of the girls' names. In an observation of classroom interactions, it became clear that I asked more questions of, and interacted with, the males more than females. The observation showed that 36% of the females in the class were asked no questions, compared with only 14% of males. A further 55% of the females were asked one question. The males were far more likely to be asked more than one question. More of an indictment is the fact that two males answered 28% of all the questions.

'In an observation of types of question asked, I found that I asked either closed, pseudo-open or control questions. The questions invariably required short answers and made little or no cognitive demand. Why did I ask such questions? I think this is probably the most important question. It is a question that I pretty much failed to ask myself during the teaching practice. The only time my questions had a clear purpose was during planned question-and-answer sessions during which pupils reported back after group work. I think that much of the rest of my questioning was a reflex action.'

Panel 5.4: A student's response to structured observation of his teaching

judgemental observation had been made criticising his questioning technique or rationale. The discomfort was generated by the student himself as he examined the data. It led him to ask, 'How can I question better?'. The answers to this question became a significant component of his action plan for his next teaching placement.

There is a considerable range of observation strategies which you can use. Ted Wragg's *An Introduction to Classroom Observation* is a useful guide that is both readable and up-to-date. It should be available in any school where students are involved.

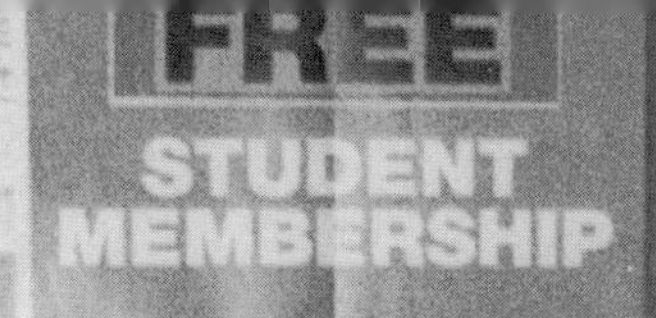

Photo: John Halocha/Adam Nichols

Chapter 6

Mentoring sessions and styles

The mentoring session is a touchstone of the mentoring process. How you conduct it will say much about you and your mentoring style. You can make it an ordeal for the student, or you can encourage thinking and growth. It is true that unproductive mentoring sessions can also be the fault of the students if they are unprepared, or unwilling to listen or to question assumptions. Nonetheless, as mentor you are the person with the power in this relationship, and the prime responsibility belongs to you.

Mentoring sessions can have a number of formats, but the common purpose should be to complete learning cycles (see Chapter 4). Normally, they will follow on from observed lessons, providing both student and mentor with an opportunity to reflect on what happened and why, and then to develop targets based on any new understanding that emerges.

This pattern of reflecting on lessons can, however, be varied:

- A session can be spent considering assessment and recording. The student may have marked books, files, essays or course work (double-marked), while the mentor can have looked at the student's comments, marks and records as a precursor to the session.
- A session might be spent on lesson and unit planning, provided that the mentor has had the opportunity to look through the student's file.
- A session may be spent reviewing the student's experience of using IT.
- A session may be spent on the broader view of teaching.

In all these variations the basis for discussion is experience, but they also utilise experience from outside the classroom, or in a different context.

There is a strong case to be made for allowing the student to comment on any observations that have been made. Some observation forms have space down the side to encourage this. Failing this layout, the students can be given the observation schedule and asked to record their responses on paper. It must be stressed that the purpose is not for the students to defend themselves (made easier if the observation is non-judgemental), but rather for them to offer their rationale for planning and executing the lesson, and to give their reaction to the observations that have been made.

Ecological analysis

This is a useful technique for encouraging students to explore the evaluative train of thinking. They are asked to see the lesson as a system with inputs, processes and outcomes (an example is given in Panel 6.1).

The analysis of lessons that went badly can often trigger fundamental thinking about planning, teaching, classroom management and pupils' learning. However, even in an analysis of what was perceived as a poor lesson, the student and mentor should also identify and analyse what went well and discuss why.

In the example shown in Panel 6.1 on the next two pages, the key points for any student are:

Ecological Analysis 9C 1/3/94 Bad Lesson

PLANNING:
Desperately wanted to make subject interesting. Thought video and worksheet would not be too boring. Wanted to try a bit of "where, what, why, when?" to see how it worked.

FEELINGS:
I had not seen this class before - had no idea what they were like or used to with their normal teacher - BIG MISTAKE!

LESSON:

1	Brief intro - S. Wales
2	Video - pick out causes of ind. loc.
3	Ideas about effects
4	Fill in work sheet W, W, W, W.

CLASS:
Mixed ability year 9. Four disruptive groups in class. Three girls not interested in work; eight boys interested in football and ink fights; three boys interested in vicious disruption techniques e.g. spitting, fighting and rest of group acting as audience.

NICE!

I was on test

Introduced myself to class and topic we would study

I knew no names and it was difficult to stop talking

Disruption started with books being handed out

Became less noisy when video was introduced

Introduced task and started video

Why di
They lo
interest

After losing interest in video the three disruptive factions became difficult to control

Hindsig

I stopped video and issued threat that if they kept up noise I would turn it off

This was particularly stupid because
- they had to see it to have somet to do that lesson and
- None were interested if I turned off anyway!

Panel 6.1: An example of ecological analysis

By the end of the video most of class were totally uninterested and must have decided that I was not at all in control

Because I was only into this by one day I did not feel confident in issuing punishments - mainly because I was unaware of the procedures. This meant that I was trying to control the class through "goodwill" alone - not punishment

In an attempt to get an orderly environment back I spent most of the last part of the lesson trying to motivate the top three antagonists

HOW

No consideration was given to those in the class who were capable of working and who wanted to work. The disruptive element took all my attention

VERY EASY MISTAKE

OUTCOMES:

1 I feel thoroughly worthless as a teacher!
2 Pupils who wished to learn did not get the opportunity.
3 I have lost important respect points which will be hard to regain.
4 Whole lesson was spent shouting and being negative.

WOULD ANYTHING MOTIVATE THE CLASS?

ACTIONS:

1 Become a postman.
2 Don't be afraid to give out sanctions
3 Try, try, try again.

- A description of the inputs to the lesson in terms of planning, feelings, characteristics of the class and (possibly) the teaching environment.
- A description of the lesson in a style that resembles a flow diagram. The events are recorded as boxes and their causes written on the connecting lines. Students are encouraged to make connections back to the inputs wherever possible, as this can unlock unsuspected lines of causation. Inevitably a personal style develops in writing these accounts.
- A statement of the outcomes of the lesson, both for the student and for the pupils, making reference both to learning and feelings.
- Finally, a statement as to what actions the student intends to take as a result of the analysis. This helps him/her to unpack the reasons behind the planning and delivery of lessons, especially if assisted by sensitive probing from the mentor.

With most students the mentoring session is best approached through open questions rather than pejorative closed questions. This should give the students confidence to question their own performance and development. When time is short, it is always tempting to 'come straight to the point', but questions which encourage reflection can make the monitoring process more effective and more efficient in the long run; consider these alternatives:

- **Direct closed criticisms/questions**
  'You didn't start that lesson very well did you?'

  'I wasn't happy with your control: you didn't have complete quiet and attention when you were giving instructions.'
- **Open questions encouraging reflection**
  'How did you feel about the lesson opening?'

  'What progress are you making in giving instructions?'

Mentoring styles

The Daloz model (Panel 6.2) gives a useful perspective on the variety of styles and roles. It has two axes: **support** and **challenge**, both of which have a high and low pole, giving four quadrants:

- high support/low challenge
- high support/high challenge
- low support/low challenge
- low support/high challenge.

As a mentor you must consider the natural style of the school and subject mentor, as well as the style that the particular student may seem most at home with. Ideally you will get to the point where you can choose what approach a particular student needs and how this might change as he/she progresses.

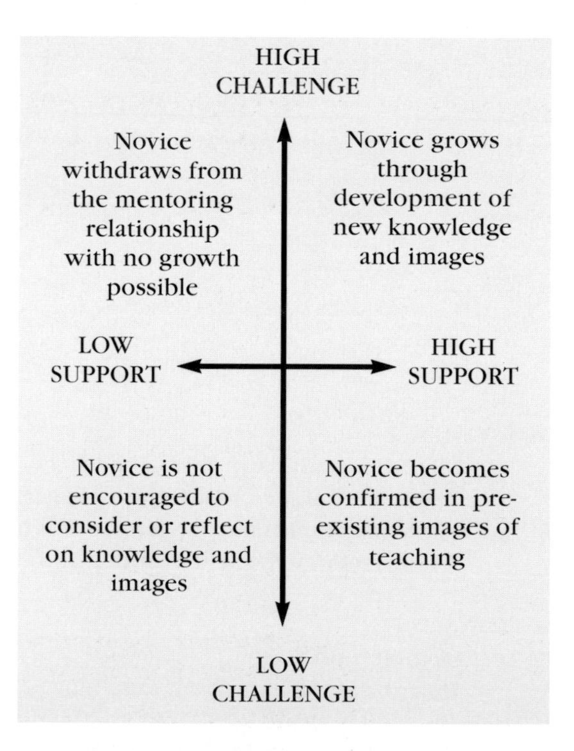

Panel 6.2: The Daloz model

'In retrospect, I learned more from being **constantly challenged** by mentors on subject content, teaching and learning styles, and classroom management, than just being left to practise my teaching skills. While practice leads to improvement, bad habits can develop very quickly. Detailed discussion based on my teaching actions and skills helped me to link theory with practice. It helped me to understand why I did certain things which increased my confidence.

'There is a need for there to be **different types of mentors** to give a broad teaching experience as well as preventing personality clashes. Having mentors from both university and school provided a lot of different information, which I am not convinced could all be taught by either institution. As well as having subject mentors to deal with lesson content and delivery, I found it most useful and interesting to have senior management mentors to provide background information on the schools. This not only opened my eyes to all the other activities going on in school, but also prevented me from becoming secluded within my department.

'One problem of having several mentors was their difference in attitude towards particular teaching and learning styles: universities seem to seek dynamic and lively lessons, whereas some schools prefer the 'chalk and talk' methods. Speaking personally, I now believe the appropriate style depends upon the teacher, the pupils and the prevailing circumstances.

'Regardless of the type of mentor (university, subject or senior management) it was reassuring to know that **encouragement and support** was available throughout. Without the help from the mentors during my teacher-training, I would not be teaching as I am now.'

Panel 6.3: A student reflects on the mentoring process

In Panel 6.3, a former PGCE student highlights the vital role played by mentors in challenging her thinking while at the same time supporting her actions. Note that being challenged is not the same as being judged!

Never be afraid to ask the question 'Why?' in mentoring sessions. Repeat it as often as necessary. This will allow you to understand the reasoning behind the lessons, and will help the students to unearth buried assumptions and priorities that may need re-examining.

Variety

There is therefore a variety of roles that mentors can play, and a range of mentoring and supervision styles. These differ in a number of important ways:

- in the extent to which the mentor values theory and the role of the HEI;
- in the extent to which the mentor thinks that learning to teach is about copying 'good' teachers or analysing practice;
- in the extent to which the mentor either just supports the students (whether passively or actively), or really stretches and challenges them.

Mentor stereotypes

One classification provides four stereotypes of school mentors:

- experienced realists
- facilitators
- protective friends
- experts.

Photo: Joanne O'Brien/Format

Experienced realists largely view the process of learning to teach as the accumulation of the knowledge and skill which they have mastered over the years. They believe that students must learn from tough classroom experience and the advice of experienced teachers on whom they can model themselves. They regard the HEI course as too theoretical and out of touch. Experienced realists are not very keen on theory and prefer the practical. They also see confidence as the key, but they choose to expose students to harsh realities rather than protecting them.

Facilitators acknowledge the element of uncertainty about teaching and accept that there are different ways of being successful. They are critical of their own teaching. They think that teachers and students can learn from each other. Their main strategy is to try to make the students think about their teaching and only to offer suggestions when requested. Facilitators are quite keen on theory, and seek to help students see teaching in a wider perspective than just their own schools. Students are regarded by facilitators as hard-working and professional.

Protective friends also have a very positive view of students, but they give less encouragement to critical reflection and are more inclined to be protective. They give a lot of personal attention and emotional support, and the blurring of the line between professionalism and friendship can become a problem. They want the students to be happy, and try to build their confidence at all costs. They will seek to protect the students, and may even defend them against critical HE tutors. Protective friends have some uncertainty about their own teaching, and some can remember to have been lacking in confidence in their own early days. They are less interested in the HE course than the facilitators, but are not critical of it.

Experts do not see teaching as an uncertain affair. They have the skills and are confident that these can be passed to the students through advice and copying. They emphasise the need for students to listen to advice and act on it. They make little attempt to allow the students to identify their agenda for development, or their interpretation of events. Experts may enjoy having students, but do not feel that they learn from them. Their main strategy is to offer definitive advice and to be there to respond to requests for advice.

'Just as every class is different and needs, to some extent, an individual approach, so every student is different.

'Some do all the reflection that is necessary and are very self-critical. The job there is to support them and help them to find a way to do what they want. With others you have to work much harder and keep on like water on a stone; they take much longer to see things.

'Another group needs help with practical things. They are full of good intentions but they don't know how to bring it off in the classroom – you have to help them to see what they have done and focus very hard on what they are doing at particular points in lessons.'

Panel 6.4: A mentor reflects on his role

If you are an effective mentor, you should be able to identify the four styles and recognise which category you tend towards. You can do this by carrying out the following three activities:

1 Consider at a personal, departmental or school level what style of mentoring you are offering. You can do this by writing down what you think you are doing for students as a mentor. If in doubt, ask the students.

2 Allocate points to the roles outlined above, depending on the emphasis that you think you give to them, and ask the students to do the same on the basis of what they think they receive.

3 Finally, consider past students and position them on the Daloz model – what combination of support and challenge did they require?

As tutors gain experience, many gain a vital overview. Panel 6.4 is an account by a school mentor (also a professional tutor), in interview, of the way he now thinks about his mentor role.

Setting targets

The process of reflecting on the quality of lessons and teaching leads naturally to the setting of targets for future lessons. These can be fairly straightforward, such as setting homework at the beginning of a lesson rather than at the end to avoid a clash with the bell. However, sometimes the target will involve difficult issues relating to the individuals' interpersonal skills. The mentor's general aim should be to probe beneath the surface so that the students can understand their own teaching performances and improve them.

Panel 6.5 highlights the importance of skilful probing. It is an account by a university PGCE tutor of two instances where the problem manifested in the classroom was a symptom of a problem located at a deeper level.

Dealing with emotions

Teaching is a profession that is practised very publicly, and learning to do it is unlike any learning that most students have experienced before. There is strong reason to believe that the emotions play a very important part in learning to teach, and there are occasions when all that seemed simple becomes complicated. Every new realisation about teaching and learning, especially where it involves a jump or change in thinking, brings an emotional cost.

Panel 6.6 is a lesson evaluation provided by a student who was struggling to motivate a low-ability year-8 class. The student was considered to be very able, and was highly thought of by all

A PGCE tutor recalls a student who complained about her performance with a low-ability year-10 group, and how it took a long time to unearth the reason.

'She had come to dislike the class because of the negative behaviour of a disaffected minority, and as a result her planning had become an exercise in control and damage limitation. Focusing on the members of the class who were positive and motivated had a significant effect on her future teaching.

'Another student had difficulty with poor transitions from one activity to another during lessons. The problem was not really with poor management planning, but in execution: in his efforts to support the work of weaker pupils, he would still be helping them through worksheet tasks when the faster ones had finished and were getting bored.'

Panel 6.5: Identifying problems and setting targets

'The class don't listen to instructions, they argue amongst themselves and generally do very little work. Two girls have been heard to say: 'I hate geography, I hate student teachers.'

'I decided to be ambitious by getting the class to investigate some photos of Brazil, introduced by some story-telling. The lesson turned out to be extremely hard work, with the pupils at their most uncooperative and tiresome.

'After the lesson I felt useless and a total failure. It felt like I couldn't teach any more. I felt scared that the class was a true reflection of my teaching ability. I was frustrated because they wouldn't let me teach them.'

Panel 6.6: Recognising the need for emotional support

concerned. Before the lesson she had felt very nervous because the three previous lessons had gone very badly.

It is obvious here that the role of the mentor in this circumstance is to support the student. There is more than enough challenge embedded in this scenario. As your experience of being a mentor develops, so will your ability to read student teachers. They will sometimes benefit from the opportunity to talk, let off steam or cry, so keep a careful eye on their moods and allow them to do this if the circumstances are right. Most emotions and feelings are better for being aired rather than bottled up. Furthermore, students who set ambitious targets which require courage may need classroom support to get them through the high-risk stage.

Conclusions

Taking responsibility for the professional learning of student teachers is an onerous task, especially as your preparation may be cursory, given all the other demands that are made on teachers. However, teachers and schools have rightly been given this responsibility, and it has to be thought about, planned for and evaluated. You should not expect to become a completely competent mentor overnight.

The effort you put into your participation in a mentoring programme should reap a number of rewards. Having students in a school and mentoring them is a chance to learn about your own professional practice (many teachers report this).

Moreover, your school should not hesitate to see students as a human resource, and you should not feel guilty that you may get some extra non-contact lessons when a student is teaching. Be pragmatic! Students can be agents for enhancing IT provision, designing new fieldwork days, initiating new course work and planning new curriculum units. They may not be experts and may not produce the finished article, but they can certainly break the back of onerous curriculum tasks. All this is some recompense for the time devoted to the system.

Photo: Joanne O'Brien/Format

Chapter 7

Three ways of helping students investigate teaching and learning

As well as being in the classroom working with pupils, students can learn about geography teaching by observing experienced teachers, by writing reflective accounts of their own experiences and by carrying out a small-scale action research project. There is plenty of scope for effective mentoring intervention in all these procedures, as this chapter shows.

1 Observing experienced teachers

Most students start their periods of school experience by observing lessons. However, teaching is not an activity which can be learned simply by watching and copying, as we saw in Chapter 4. This is partly because each lesson is a unique event, and partly because the interactions taking place in an experienced teacher's lessons are strongly influenced by previous, unseen lessons. So the aim of including classroom observation in any programme for beginner teachers is not so that they can simply copy what they see, but so that they can become more aware of the complexity of what is going on. This will naturally increase their understanding of classroom processes and decisions (Walker 1985).

It is not uncommon for students to become bored watching lessons; most want to get 'stuck in' themselves. So it is important that you help them to see the point of observing. The following case study of structured and directed observation is a good example of this.

Background

In the first phase of their course, student teachers spent three days per week in university-based activities and two days per week in school. The activities relate to a sequence of topics about teaching geography and are planned and evaluated jointly by university tutors and school mentors. The activity aims to help students increase their awareness and understanding of:

- how a geography teacher can recognise and take account of pupil differences;
- the differences between pupils, in particular with regard to the nature of individual learning needs and achievements within a class;
- the demands made on pupils by different teaching strategies;
- some of the different teaching strategies which can be implemented in the geography classroom.

Preliminary activities in the university

A simple exercise introducing origami put most students in a new learning situation. The debriefing discussion highlighted individual differences in learning patterns, which can be categorised in a similar way to those identified in school:

- cognitive
- practical
- emotional
- behavioural.

The tutor then briefly referred to national policy developments, and emphasised the value of the process of identifying students' needs, investigating their nature, making provision, and then reviewing each step in the process.

In a small-group exercise students were asked to reflect about their previous school experience as a means of identifying their current thinking about general and geographical learning difficulties and achievements.

Whole-group discussion allowed students to share their experiences. This was followed by a tutor summary of research and writing in this area.

In a small-group exercise students were asked to analyse a range of textbooks in order to create a summary of student tasks which appeared to meet the learning needs previously identified.

In a concluding exercise pairs of students were asked to develop sets of questions about classroom observation, for discussion with their mentors in school over the next two days.

Activities in the partnership school

Having observed the mentor teaching one or more lessons, students were allocated the following tasks:

- during the initial observation, to focus on two pupils with different levels of achievement;
- to note the pupils' individual learning needs and achievements;
- to note their mentor's teaching strategies, especially as they affected the selected pupils.

After discussing their observations with the mentor, they were then asked to discover:

- the rationale adopted by their mentor;
- the rationale adopted by the geography department for teaching mixed-ability classes.

Follow-up activities

Back at the university, the students worked in groups from different schools to share the results and then to summarise teaching strategies which they could use in mixed-ability classes.

Further activities in school and university explored:

- the needs of able pupils in geography;
- lesson planning for mixed-ability classes;
- guided teaching experience for the students themselves with mixed-ability classes.

The observed lesson

The aims of the mentor's lesson were to help a class of mixed-ability key stage 3 pupils to understand the difficulties of portraying the globe as a map, and to appreciate the properties of different projections.

Pupils' work consisted of three main activities:

- answering a series of questions asked by the mentor about the properties of a number of world maps, shown as overhead transparencies;
- constructing a globe from a supplied outline;
- for homework, answering written questions about the properties of different world maps.

After the lesson

After the lesson, the student and mentor had a discussion session. Here are some of the main points raised:

Pupil A

The student commented on Pupil A that in the first part of the lesson her main difficulty seemed to be in concentrating and that she didn't look to be very involved. She had her head in her hands, and at one point began talking to a neighbour. However, she did offer to answer one of the teacher's questions. In the second part of the lesson, she did concentrate, she did not need much help and when the teacher asked her how she was doing she said 'fine'. She got on well with the exercise, finished the task, and didn't make any mistakes in colouring, cutting or sticking the globe together. She achieved very well.

The student hadn't noticed the mentor employing any particular strategies with this pupil, who seemed to be getting on well with the task and needed no extra help.

The mentor agreed that this pupil often had great difficulty in concentrating, although it was not easy to observe this because she was generally quiet in class and consequently her inattention was rarely reflected in her behaviour. He said that he often moved the pupil to work on her own, as he had found that she worked well in this situation. He thought the pupil had a creative mind, and often produced 'really good ideas, an alternative viewpoint' especially in written work.

Pupil B

The student noted that in the first part of the lesson, Pupil B had had problems in concentration, and spent a lot of time looking at the OHP rather than at the screen. He hadn't offered to answer any questions but hadn't disrupted the lesson. In the second part of the lesson, he had problems understanding the maps - for example, in identifying countries, and comparing the size and shape of the same country on different maps. He had needed considerable help from the mentor, but he had completed the task and asked to take his globe home.

The student described some of the ways in which the mentor had worked with this pupil. He had frequently spent time with him, giving him a new map when he had made a mistake on the first. He had helped the pupil considerably towards the end of the lesson, as he had seemed to be getting frustrated with the practical task and had been talking about things outside the lesson.

The mentor agreed that this pupil had difficulty in concentrating and understanding: 'Much of the information goes over his head. He looks as though he's listening, but often doesn't understand.' He emphasised that he had given instructions for the practical exercise both orally and written on the board. He thought 98% of the class could understand the instructions and carry them out, but said that he always had to explain any task to Pupil B before he could begin to do the work. He said this pupil would always try very hard and would never misbehave. He pointed out that 'the reason why he carried on colouring the sea was because the longer it took, the longer it was before he got into real difficulty.'

One of the students had asked a learning support teacher about this pupil. The teacher said that Pupil B always took a long time to understand instructions and to learn anything, and that he had extreme learning difficulties, especially with reading and writing.

PGCE student's comment on the value of the activity

'Just realising how complex learning difficulties are, and that you can't just say 'these are the low achievers and these are the high achievers.' Because if you observe a variety of tasks in mixed-ability teaching, that's one way as a beginning teacher that you can try to understand learning difficulties. With somebody like Pupil A, if you did have a lesson which was based on written work, or quite traditional in the sense of talking a lot to the class, then she would seem to be someone who had problems with concentration, and with motivation and attitude problems, so she might become a difficult pupil. But if you then have a more practical lesson, she then becomes a much more diligent, achieving pupil. So I did find it useful ...

'... focusing on two pupils was really good because I realised you can never do that when you're teaching ... you could see exactly where their concentration lapsed and came in. You could really work out how they interacted with other pupils. Later, I spoke to the learning support teacher about learning difficulties, and I learned a lot from that.'

The mentor's viewpoint

'Now I've always thought that one of the greatest difficulties in teaching is teaching mixed-ability classes with pupils with learning difficulties. Planning is the key to this - making sure that you've got a variety of tasks, careful explanation, hands-on tasks, a bit of groupwork. This activity does make you think about the principles of teaching mixed ability ... when I knew I was going to do this lesson, I did really think about how I was going to involve the class. I know most of the time I am aware of this, but obviously sometimes it kind of slips by the wayside with teaching all the other classes. So just trying to focus on principles and making sure that there's something for everybody in this lesson was good for me.

'I think that you would learn from seeing how the pupils reacted in different sections of the lesson. So the first section was quite specifically me talking and them answering questions, and no one was to speak unless their hands were up. They were focused on me and the OHT. They were meant to be quiet and you can see that some of them cannot handle being quiet - cannot sit still.

'By specifying observation and understanding, particularly of the difficulties, you can think of strategies, and in particular how to enable each pupil to learn. So it's by looking at individual pupils and saying 'That pupil needs this' that you can see where the failings were in the lesson.

'You can often make the mistake of looking at the class as a single unit. We talk about the class - "They do this", "They do that" or "They were difficult" - but we often forget about individuals ... I'm always learning as well ... and that's why it helps me to think about the individuals and how they respond.

'It's good to look at Pupil A and Pupil B and whoever, but with the next lot of pupils you look at there'll be different problems again. If you've got a bank of strategies, then you can try out something similar.'

The university tutor's comments on the value of the activity

'This programme, in addition to the specific aims listed above, helps students in ways which will benefit their continuing professional development. These include:

- observation of pupils and teachers in lessons;
- discussion with teachers about teaching and learning - opportunities to think about and evaluate their own pre-conceptions and existing experiences;
- sharing ideas with other PGCE students who may have different preconceptions and school experiences;
- learning about aspects of national policy, and about research on teaching and learning.

'The sequence of structured activities described above is only possible if school mentors and university tutors know the contributions which each can make most effectively, and this does depend on a high level of collaboration between them.'

Comments on observation case study

This extended case study illustrates several characteristics of successful, purposeful observation of experienced teachers:

1 It was tightly focused on a particular issue. Focused observation is much better than a general requirement just to watch a particular lesson.

2 The issue was related to the student teachers' own experiences. Students bring to their training expectations of classrooms, based on their own experiences and their own values. Prior knowledge affects how observers interpret what they see and how they judge it.

3 The observation was related to issues beyond this particular school. There is an important role for higher education in any partnership, helping students to make sense of a particular classroom in a wider context, which would include national policy.

4 The students discussed how and what they were going to observe. They were not merely carrying out the mentor's or the tutor's instructions. They had chance to shape the activity to meet their needs.

5 The follow-up activities provided additional motivation. They knew that they would be able to discuss what they had observed with the experienced teacher and to raise any questions about it. Such discussion helps the student to see the lesson from the teacher's perspective rather than the pupil's perspective – something which some students find difficult at the start of a PGCE course. They were also aware that they would soon be teaching some mixed-ability classes.

6 The value of the observation was increased by the HEI tutor providing a structured opportunity for students to share their observation of different pupils, classes and schools with each other. This would add to the repertoire they would be able to draw upon in dealing with unique situations.

2 Reflective writing

Apart from observation, another way of helping students to learn from experience is by encouraging reflective writing. Of course, they will use several other kinds of writing during their teacher training. For example, writing essays encourages reading about issues and thinking about them beyond the context of the schools in which students work; writing reports on issues should develop the ability to write clearly and succinctly, while writing lesson plans will help them to structure their thoughts.

Reflective writing is more personal, and encourages students to explore their experiences in relation to their feelings and assumptions. It can be a means of exploring new, sometimes puzzling and threatening situations. It is more tentative than essay or report writing and reveals the dilemmas which teachers face. It can reveal the student teacher's thinking *during* a lesson and thinking *after* a lesson (Schon 1983).

Because of the learning potential of written reflection, many teacher-training courses encourage students to write personal accounts, diaries and journals. The following case study describes an example of an assignment encouraging reflective writing. It is based on students working with the university tutor, two geography mentors and year-10 pupils on a residential field visit to Coniston. An account of the broader aspects of using this fieldwork in a teacher-education context is given by Butt (1995).

Background

The HEI course includes a one-week residential field study with children from a partnership school. Before this takes place, student teachers liaise with the geography department of the school to seek guidance about the planning of the fieldwork. Two geography teachers (one a trained mentor) and a university tutor accompany the student teachers on the field study to provide support during this first experience of running residential work.

After the field study, a written report is produced by each student teacher. This must be 'A critical account of a field course at Coniston with special reference to planning, organisation, aims and objectives, field methods, expected outcomes and actual outcomes'.

The report attempts to make the writer reflect upon his or her experience of working with a small group to organise and lead a day's field activities. Students are directed to comment upon their own and other people's organisational and teaching skills in an honest and open way, offering suggestions for possible alternatives to these approaches. During the week, there are regular discussion sessions. The experience of understanding practical field teaching, and then reflecting upon it with peers, a mentor, and the university tutor, certainly helps the process of writing the assignment.

Thus, although the written assignment is a summative account, much of its concern arises from more immediate and formative evaluations carried out during the field-study week itself. Informal comments made by the tutor, mentor, other students and pupils during the week are part of this. Video recordings of teaching in the field, and back at the field-study centre, have also been used in the past to evaluate teaching quality.

Extract from a student's report

The following extract, taken from a student's report, illustrates the first steps taken by a group of three students to initiate some field activities with a group of pupils:

'This was the first day of the fieldwork. Although we had arrived on Sunday, the pupils didn't arrive until early on the Monday afternoon, so by the time they arrived to do my group's fieldwork they had been travelling for about four hours and were pretty tired, to say the least. This was something which I found quite difficult, for I didn't really want to start talking to the pupils straight away about the fieldwork we had set up. This is where good teamwork came in handy!

'Martin took over to 'break the ice' by getting everyone settled and introducing the student teachers in our team, and telling the pupils which students they would be with. This worked really well because the pupils relaxed, and it gave me a chance to scan the room, take in details and start to make eye contact - which is always so hard to do if you just walk straight into a room full of unknown children.

'Seeing as we had to do a fair amount of walking and would be stopping to work, I tried not to go over organisational things in too much detail to start with, and to keep it brief, clear and punchy. I think that in places this may have come out as too didactic, and it was not a very pupil-centred briefing. I was so busy trying to get pupils out into the field that I didn't think to involve them more - even if it had been a quick question-and-answer session.

'It had been a factor of great importance to our group that we should really emphasise the safety aspect of being out in the field, and Claire, Martin and myself did this once or twice to the whole group and individually throughout the exercise. There were certain rules which we made sure all pupils adhered to. For example, none of them were allowed to go right down to the lake shore. This worked very well and all pupils kept to the safety guidelines we had given them.'

The student's comment on the assignment

'The practice of reflecting on one's work is integral to all parts of the course and is an approach which should stay with teachers throughout their careers. During the Geography PGCE, critical self-evaluation tends to become part of life, but there are some spheres of teaching in which the student tends to realise its value more than others, and one of these has to be field study. It is essential that student teachers are aware of the education and care of their pupils outside the classroom. This, of course, can only be learned through personal experience and then reflection. This is why field study should be an important part of the Geography PGCE. It gives the student teacher a chance to encounter all the major pitfalls of out-of-class activities without taking the ultimate responsibilities!

'The reflective written assignment gives the student teachers a further chance to learn from their first hand experiences. It highlights the individual's strengths and weaknesses when working with children in the field, and gives you the confidence to build upon those experiences.'

The mentor's comment on the assignment

'The week of residential field study has considerable advantages for all concerned. For the student teachers it provides excellent teaching experience, and involves fieldwork planning and organisation under supervision. This is particularly important for fieldwork undertaken with year-10 and year-11 pupils, whose field-study reports can form the whole, or part, of the course-work requirement for GCSE Geography. A residential experience is, in itself, a teaching and learning experience. The very high ratio of staff/students to pupils can encourage innovation and a sense of confidence in learning from others. Team planning and team teaching are clear learning experiences which will be of use to the student teachers in their future careers.

'The writing of a reflective assignment seems to have several benefits, given the range of different activities expected of the student teachers during this week. The first field activity carried out by the students was a decision-making exercise, *Siting of a Leisure Centre*, which proved to be a good starting point for a number of reasons. A safe rural environment, very different from the pupils' own, was used to generate an activity whereby children could get into the field quickly after their long journey. The overall aim of the field study (to examine *Conflicts of Interest within a National Park*) was focused upon, and the activity set the pattern of working for the rest of the week. During their planning of activities, student teachers also had to think about evening follow-up work, including role play, group discussion and decision making. The use of video, both while recording in the field and during follow-up sessions, provided a very useful feedback to pupils, students, and staff, and was also an effective teaching and learning tool back in school.'

Comment by the university tutor

'The process of writing a reflective assignment on the planning, organisation and teaching of field study seems to me a valuable one for a variety of reasons.

'Firstly, it encourages student teachers to evaluate their own practice – a task which is essential in the initial phases of teaching, but also important if one is to carry on advancing in terms of pedagogy.

'Secondly, it attempts to make students consider the teaching of others – usually that of other students whom they have not seen teach before, but also that of their university tutor and mentor. Comments, be they positive or negative, have to be justified, and the reasons why the student thinks a particular field activity or debriefing session was successful (or not!) have to be stated. This often encourages the students to consider teaching techniques and approaches which they have not experienced previously, or have thought to be too difficult or 'not for them'. Therefore, many students return from the field-study week with a number of ideas about how they can enhance their repertoires of teaching skills.

'Lastly, the process of writing a reflective assignment is, in itself, a learning experience which clarifies thoughts and ideas.

'Apparent within the extract from the student's assignment, which considers the first steps towards fieldwork, is an initial and understandable apprehension about working with children she does not yet know, and who are tired from a long journey to an unfamiliar destination. She evaluates her own approach and acknowledges the advantages of being able to work within a group of teachers to overcome some of these difficulties, noting points such as the importance of establishing eye contact with the children during the initial briefing. Although she considers her own practice to be 'too didactic' and 'not very pupil-centred', this is qualified by her comment that she was in a rush to get the pupils into the field. Importantly, she realises a solution to these difficulties within this context - such as the use of a 'quick question-and-answer session'.

'The comments which she makes within this extract are not only straightforward and practical, but reveal a process of reflection, evaluation and thought that should be part of any teacher's development.'

Comments on reflective writing case study

This case study illustrates some of the circumstances in which reflective writing can be very valuable:

1 The residential visit was an intense experience for the student teachers. The students were with the pupils continuously for five days. They were teaching in a potentially dangerous environment. They were required to be in charge of activities and to teach in front of their peers, their tutor and two mentors. Although it was an enjoyable experience, it was potentially stressful. Reflective writing is a way of exploring intense experiences such as this or other intense situations, e.g. first lessons with classes, lessons which developed in an unpredicted way, highly successful lessons and unsuccessful lessons.

2 There was a lot of discussion of what happened during the field visit, both informally and formally, in evening sessions. Reflective writing is stimulated by discussion; writing can take the thinking further and help the writer to sort out ideas and feelings. It can help students explore what they have learned from the experience.

3 The students felt free to voice their doubts and their uncertainties and to be self-critical. The tutor welcomed openness and honesty. He was in a better position to support their professional development by knowing what dilemmas they faced and the feelings behind their actions. Reflective writing is supported by being received in an open and sympathetic way.

3 Action research

Action research has been promoted since the 1970s as a way of enabling teachers to promote their own professional development; Stenhouse (1975) wrote about 'teachers as researchers'. Although most action research has been carried out by experienced teachers investigating some aspect of their practice or evaluating some curriculum innovation, it can be also be a valuable way of helping student teachers to develop their professional skills. A small-scale piece of action research is our third example of ways of enabling students to investigate the processes of teaching and learning.

Action research has the aim of changing or improving practice rather than generating theoretical knowledge or generalisations (Elliott 1991). It is cyclical, with several phases:

1 **Planning** - identifying the general idea to be researched, planning the activity to be researched, and planning the research itself.

2 **Action and monitoring** - carrying out what is being researched, e.g. teaching a lesson and collecting research data, often through observation.

3 **Reflection** - analysing the data, interpreting the data, evaluating the 'action'.

4 **Re-planning** - revising the action in light of the research ... and repeating the cycle.

The cycle can be repeated several times. The following extended case study concentrating on observation and analysis of classroom interaction illustrates a way in which student teachers can be guided through the sequence for the first time.

The context

During the PGCE course, geography students complete four curriculum assignments during the year. One of these is based on observations carried out during the first period of block school experience in November and December. To complete this assignment the students work in pairs in partnership schools, and observe each other as part of a peer-support system.

The assignment

'Classroom interaction: an enquiry into your own classroom practice' - to include:

- extracts from the guidelines for the assignment;
- asking your teaching-practice partner to observe one of your lessons ...
- the focus for enquiry - decide what you want to have observed;
- the data for enquiry - decide on a methodology and discuss with your partner how to collect data in your lesson;
- analysis of data - collect the data from your partner, making sure you understand
    - the data collected
    - what happened during the lesson
    - whether there were any patterns of interaction;
- explanation - how do you explain what happened in your lesson, and to what extent have the patterns observed in your own lessons been observed by other researchers?
- evaluation of the lesson;
- evaluation of the enquiry.

Carrying out the assignment

Students choose various aspects of interaction as a focus for observation, such as:

- Which pupils in the class do I give little attention to and why?
- Do I interact differently with boys and girls?
- What kind of attention and support do I give to those with special educational needs, including both those with learning difficulties and those who

Photo: Imogen Young/Format

need additional challenges?

- What kinds of questions do I ask in lessons?
- What patterns of praise and criticism are there in my lessons?

Sometimes the focus arises from a remark made by the school mentor about a lesson, sometimes from interests arising from prior experience or from reading. After reading about classroom research, students consider how to investigate their particular questions. They work collaboratively with their partners, taking turns at observing and being observed. Their written reports average 3000 words.

Comments of PGCE students on their enquiries
(taken from their reports)

- 'Observation is definitely a worthwhile experience and makes you more aware of things that are happening within the classroom. It needs an objective observer to notice the occurrences that the teacher misses and passes over.'
- 'This study has proved interesting and

allowed me the opportunity to stand back and look at how I teach, my weaknesses, strengths and possible and necessary areas for improvement. Decisions concerning classroom control in particular are largely spontaneous, but there is still room for thought.'

- 'The observation and evaluation of this one lesson has proved an invaluable starting point for my development as a more positive teacher.'
- 'This enquiry has succeeded in its aim of heightening my awareness of the problems created by gender stereotyping ... I can appreciate how easy it is to form stereotypes subconsciously. On a purely personal level, I found this enquiry immensely interesting. It has succeeded in making me review my attitudes towards boys and girls and my expectations of them.'
- 'I realised how I had effectively missed out most of those who sit at the front of the class for half of the lesson.'
- 'I will be making more of an effort to spend more time with the girls even if they don't request it.'
- 'It did provide some insight into my classroom practice in that there did appear to be some gender imbalance in the classroom interaction. More importantly, however, I feel this enquiry holds more significance in the whole learning process of teacher training. This is because it is another means to encourage you to examine your teaching behaviour in the classroom and employ self-assessment and explanation. Also I found it important as an introduction to classroom research ... which will prove invaluable when reading educational literature in the future.'
- 'Despite the drawbacks and limitations, the study has done much to link my real world of teaching practice to the theory contained in the literature. This has provided a valuable starting point for the understanding of the processes at work in the classroom.'
- 'Was this enquiry useful? Definitely yes!'

Comments from one of the geography mentors

'With two students in the classroom there is a tremendous opportunity for researching classroom interaction and reflecting on pedagogy. The assignment encourages student teachers to become self-critical and to raise their awareness of issues of classroom dynamics they might otherwise encounter only through the theoretical literature.

'Moreover, in encouraging student teachers to design their own enquiries into classroom interaction, by deciding on what they intend to observe and how they intend to collect and analyse the data, they are forced to think very deeply about the issues of interaction in the classroom, and in particular the role of the teacher in affecting patterns of interaction in the classroom. It also encourages student teachers to delve into the educational literature and relate their findings to other research.

'From a school point of view, discussion of their findings with teachers in the department enthuses and encourages experienced teachers to see their own practice in a new light. Perhaps, most importantly, it fosters the long-term perspective that all teachers, no matter how long they have been teaching, should continually analyse and research the effects of what they are doing in the classroom.'

Comments of the HEI tutor

'This assignment allows students to focus on what is of most concern to them. The focus does not have to be related to geography, but the observations take place in geography lessons. I would argue that the way in which teachers interact with pupils in the classroom, and the patterns of interactions, have a strong influence on each individual pupil's learning of geography.

'The extracts quoted above from the student assignments illustrate the different ways in which the close observation of just one lesson was valuable to different students. There was increased awareness of what was happening in the classroom; assessment of practice; increased understanding of processes; awareness of the influence of subconscious attitudes; reflection on the spontaneity of actions in the classroom; introduction to the research literature; pointers to future action; and provision of a methodology of investigating one's teaching in future.

Students gained from observing and being observed. Although the investigation was small-scale and, as most students point out, could not produce valid generalisations, it provided useful insights. A number of students wrote about the experience as 'a starting point' for professional development – an interesting comment on an assignment completed *after* several weeks of classroom practice.'

Comments on the action research case study

The students, within the framework provided by an assignment, decided on their own focus for research. They were investigating something they wanted to find out. Student investigations are more meaningful if they are meeting the students' needs.

The students had already worked in pairs in the classroom for some of their lessons. They now had someone available to collect information – a partner in research. Peer observation is one of many valuable ways of using two students in the classroom.

The teaching-practice partner was used for initial discussion of the data. This helped initial interpretation and exploration of the issues. The collaborative nature of peer observation, with each student taking a turn at being observer and observed, is likely to lead to an understanding, sympathetic approach, with each student sensitive to the feelings of the other.

The action research was guided and enhanced by the students' wider reading. This enabled them to place their small study into a wider context and to become aware of ways of researching their own practice in future. Students benefit more from wider reading when they can relate it to their own practice.

The students in this case were likely to change their classroom practice as a result of just one lesson's close observation and reflection on it, even if they do not complete another cycle of action research. Action research can give the student teacher some control over his or her professional development and improvement. Ultimately, this method of self-improvement is preferable to their depending on being told how to improve by a tutor or mentor; it points a way to continued professional development after the initial training course.

Summing up partnership-based training

Each of these three case studies is an example of close co-operation between schools and higher education which provides students with learning activities beyond the classroom itself. None of the activities could be described as being examples of school-based training or of university-based training. They are all excellent examples of *partnership-based training* in which the students make use of the context the school can provide, plus the expertise of experienced teachers working within that context, and what higher education can provide (i.e. a broader view of the context, informed by wider knowledge of national issues and educational research and the opportunity for large groups of students to share their experiences). The case studies have presented the student teachers' course as part of an ongoing process of professional development, rather than mainly as a means of gaining initial competence, important though this is. In each of these cases the mentors and tutors were also learning and developing their understanding of geographical education.

Photo: John Halocha/Adam Nichols

Bibliography

Specific references

Barker, S. *et al.* (1995), *Initial teacher education in secondary schools*, Warwick: Institute of Education, University of Warwick and the Association of Teachers and Lecturers.

Berliner, D. C. (1987), 'Ways of thinking about students and more and less experienced teachers', in Calderhead, J. (ed.), *Exploring teachers' thinking*, London: Cassell.

Butt, G. (1995), 'Residential field study within a partnership framework', in Williams, A. (ed.), *Partnership in secondary initial teacher education*, London: David Fulton, pp. 25-38.

Calderhead, J. and Robson, M. (1991), 'Images of teaching: Student teachers' early conceptions of classroom practice', *Teaching and Teacher Education*, 7, pp. 1-8.

DFE (1992), *Reform of initial teacher training (secondary)*, Circular 9/92.

Elliott, J. (1991), *Action Research for Educational Change*, Milton Keynes: Open University.

Elliott, J. (1991), 'A model of professionalism and its implications for teacher education', *British Educational Research Journal*, 17, pp. 309-319.

Ellis, B. (1993), 'Training geography teachers: An increased role for schools', *Teaching Geography*, 18(3), pp. 129-131.

Foskett, N. (1994), 'What are we going to do with our student teacher?', *Teaching Geography*, 19(1), pp. 26-29.

Fuller, F. F. and Bown, O. H. (1975), 'Becoming a teacher', in Ryan, K. (ed.), *Teacher Education* (74th Yearbook of the National Society for the Study of Education, II), Chicago: University of Chicago, pp. 25-52.

Hughes, M. (1994), 'School-based teacher training: Like learning through fieldwork', *Teaching Geography*, 19(4), pp. 171-174.

Ince, C. (1994), 'Appointing newly-qualified mature geography teachers', *Teaching Geography*, 19(2), pp. 81-83.

Kolb, D. (1984), *Experiential Learning*, Englewood Cliffs, NJ: Prentice Hall.

McPartland, M. (1995), 'On being a geography mentor', *Teaching Geography*, 20(1), pp. 35-38.

Schon, D. (1983), *The Reflective Practitioner*, London: Temple Smith.

Stenhouse, L. (1975), *An introduction to curriculum research and development*, London: Heinemann.

TTA (1997), *Standards for the Award of Qualified Teacher Status*, London: Teacher Training Agency.

Walker, R. (1985), *Doing research: A handbook for teachers*, London: Methuen.

Wragg, E. C. (1994), *An Introduction to Classroom Observation*, London: Routledge.

General texts

Fish, D. (ed.) (1995), *Quality learning for student teachers: University tutors' educational practices*, London: David Fulton.

Fish, D. (ed.) (1995), *Quality mentoring for student teachers: A principled approach to practice*, London: David Fulton.

Tolley, H., Biddulph, M. and Fisher, T. (1996), *The professional development management file*, Cambridge: Chris Kington.

The last is a more elaborated series of tasks and activities for the professional development of teachers at all stages of their careers, and includes the following workbooks:

- 'Pre-entry to initial teacher training'
- 'Beginning initial teacher training'
- 'Block teaching practice'
- 'Pre-entry to first teaching post'
- 'The first year of teaching'
- 'Beyond the first year of teaching'.